Building Wealth in a Paycheck-to-Paycheck World

Building Wealth in a Paycheck-to-Paycheck World

10 Steps to Realizing Your Dream No Matter What You Earn

Paul Petillo

McGraw-Hill

New York   Chicago   San Francisco   Lisbon   London
Madrid   Mexico City   Milan   New Delhi
San Juan   Seoul   Singapore   Sydney   Toronto

1 2 3 4 5 6 7 8 9 0 DOC/DOC 0 9 8 7 6 5 4

ISBN 0-07-142376-1

This publication is designed to provide accurate and authoritative information in regard to the subject matter covered. It is sold with the understanding that the publisher is not engaged in rendering legal, accounting or other professional services. If legal advice or other expert assistance is required, the services of a competent professional person should be sought.
>   —*From a Declaration of Principles Jointly Adapted by a Committee of the*
>   *American Bar Association and a Committee of Publishers and Associations.*

McGraw-Hill books are available at special quantity discounts to use as premiums and sales promotions, or for use in corporate training programs. For more information, please write to the Director of Special Sales, McGraw-Hill Professional, Two Penn Plaza, New York, NY 10121-2298. Or contact your local bookstore.

This book is printed on recycled, acid-free paper containing a minimum of 50% recycled, de-inked fiber.

*To Bon, my wife of twenty years,
the person I run to at the end of the day.
I love you.*

Contents

Preface

Hamburger to Caviar

Both Ben and Charles Darwin and, in a rudimentary way, early humans were aware of the Bayes' rule. You probably have never heard of it, although I'd be willing to wager that you practice it in some way every day.

Steve Slavik and I coached a grade school CYO basketball team for a good many years. Ben was one of our players, a handsome young man whose confidence seemed to ooze from every pore. He was the kind of kid who had good basketball skills and knew it. He would make a move to the hoop and would appear to be making a highlight film in his head as if he could see himself in some sort of out-of-body way. Or perhaps, as Thomas Bayes, an eighteenth-century British mathematician once theorized, Ben was relying on what he knew as he did what he could see. Bayes' rule suggests that we draw on these experiences, the memories we gather and collect throughout our lives, to make everyday decisions.

I was watching a special on the Discovery Channel that dealt with early humans. The creators of the show did a great job making these digitally reproduced savage and hairy scavengers appear real.

The show suggested that every skill or insight these early humans developed was based on some experience. When digitally reproduced animals attacked them, the group was left with a new piece of information. Each time they experienced something new, they, with the advantage of

their ever-increasing brains, made a mental note. This was the anthropo-
logical birth of Bayes' rule.

Charles Darwin was famous for taking notes as a response to this brain
function. He did this not because he was forgetful but because he knew
something fundamental about himself. He understood that if he stumbled
upon something that contradicted a belief he held close, he was inclined to
try and disprove it. In other words, he would talk himself out of what his
eyes could plainly see. To guard against this tendency, therefore, he would
write down his observations. These notes wouldn't allow him to reject whatever he had just experienced, even after he had time to think about it.

This book will be your note. This is where we will sort through all
your financial experiences. Together, we will put them in one basket, sift
through them, and try to determine what they mean. We will look at the
obvious and attempt to understand the importance of what you might have
missed. Once we arrive at that point, we will be able to move on, making
our own conclusions based on more than simply what we believe.

Overcoming the Bayes' rule will not be easy. Mr. Bayes understood
that simple acts such as crossing a busy street would require that you can
not only comprehend what is in front of you but also make estimates of
other factors in the scene. Past memories of a car's speed would play an
important role in your decision concerning the safest time to cross.

So Ben, who knew that he could make the shot during the game
because he had practiced it repeatedly at home in his driveway, drew on
his experience to give him the confidence he needed; like those early
ancestors of ours who knew the ferocity of an attacking animal or the
effects of a new-found berry, so they learned something new while at
the same time recalling what they already knew; and like Darwin scrib-
bling notes that allowed him to sharpen his focus so that he could learn
without permitting his brain to cloud his view with previous experiences,
we are going to do much the same thing here. It is, for many of us, those
past experiences that are at the heart of our financial decisions.

Over the course of five years, I have run two financially based Web
sites and newsletters. The people I write for and those who have written
back are just like you and me. They live and work in a world very similar
to yours. It is people like us who frustrate policymakers in Washington,
economists, and academics who study our behavior.

No two people are alike. I never realized this until after the tragedy that occurred on September 11, 2001. The *New York Times* ran a series that encapsulated the lives of each victim of that terror attack. Each and every one of those unfortunate souls had something unique and at the same time familiar to every one of us. They came from similar walks of life, places we could identify with, and lives that had relevance to the folks around them. They converged daily on a place, bringing with them each and every fabric of their experience and sharing them with others.

As individual as we are, we share many of the same experiences. We all share similar pleasures and common pains. We have children, and we have none. We are born in different parts of the world, but we have a lot in common. We are colored differently, and yet we all are made of the same biological stuff. We live, and some of us die.

In the end, we all live, play, and work. In fact, we work far too much, play far too little, and live without giving it all that much thought. And we take far too few mental notes.

The experience of creating and writing a Web site such as *BlueCollarDollar.com* has been a richly rewarding endeavor that brought every little "note to self" onto the screens of hundreds of thousands of readers. I set out to teach but found instead that I was to learn even more. By opening up my thoughts, I was inviting the responses of readers. What prompted these people to write those short e-mails or lengthy dissertations about their lives? Was it my material, my fiery delivery, or my ability to bend words to my will? Or perhaps it was something entirely different. Most of their letters contained words of desperation, their inability to grasp the world of money, or envy of those who had achieved wealth.

I went from a financial writer to an economic behaviorist and never even realized it. What I have found, and I admit that I am excited by the idea, is that we are far better off than we understand. That's right. We fail to understand why we should be happy. We should be forward-thinking and optimistic, understanding that wealth is a how, not a who or a what.

Daniel Kahneman is a psychology professor at Princeton University. He has been there for the last decade. The Royal Swedish Academy of Sciences awarded him the Nobel Prize for Economics "for having integrated insights from psychological research into economic science, especially concerning human judgment and decision making under uncertainty." What all this means is that he discovered how people like you and me depart from the predictable to do the unexplainable. In the process, he created a new field of research.

Before he published his thoughts, there was a belief that rich people always felt good and poor people always felt bad. It was this driving belief, especially when held by "poor" people, that kept us thinking that we can better our lot in life. We believe that one day we can "make it." Whether through hard work, perseverance, and fortitude or just through a simple twist of luck, we, deep down in our hearts, believe that we can ride in limos, dine expensively, and live luxuriously. Each and every one of us knows exactly what we would do with wealth. We know how we would spend it, whom we would spend it on, and where we would go. Some of us have made those elaborate scenarios seem attainable.

Who of us hasn't stood in line when the lottery jackpot has reached eight or nine figures, creating "wealth dreams" beyond our imaginations? Who among us hasn't drifted off to sleep divvying up that fortune among their children and loved ones, creating comfort and privilege?

This book could be a book of dreams. I think that you will find it to be more of a turning point in time where you just might find something that will motivate you to go beyond simply thinking about changing your financial present and actually doing something. It will, I hope, motivate you into actually doing something about the only future you get.

Back to Mr. Kahneman. What the good professor found was that the experience of finding $10 would be the same for a well-to-do person as for someone less well-off. The condition would, even if momentarily, give both pleasure. So why do we tend to separate these two groups, the rich and the not-so-rich, as if they existed in worlds so different that they are beyond each other's understanding?

On the flip side, if we both feel pleasure, then we both feel pain as well. This may, for some who strive to become wealthy one day, arrive as a shock. From the depths of our financial despair, we all imagine that wealth is a place without discomfort. The ability to surround oneself with luxuries can only increase the pleasure. We do this even when we know that pleasure is a condition, not some sort of level.

The belief that money makes everything better is wholly untrue. What it does do is make it more comfortable. Whenever you feel pleasure, you feel as though your condition is better. You feel pain when you suffer some sort of loss, whether it is personal or financial. No matter how much money you have, you feel the same sort of pain. The emotion doesn't change with monetary worth. Researchers have found that loss at any income level can be very real and very painful.

In other words, your condition, if it makes you happy, will likewise give you pleasure, no matter who you are.

Some will argue that caviar tastes better than hamburger. Having wealth, I'm afraid, doesn't make food taste differently. Understanding wealth, however, changes everything.

Acknowledgments

I want to thank the following people for believing in me. If they thought I was crazy for trying, they were nice enough to never say so . . . at least to my face.

To the guys in Bend, Oregon, Andre Jensen, Derrick Wheeler, and Marshall Simmonds, who helped me build the *BlueCollarDollar.com* with insightful and sage advice. While they forced me to do all of the work myself, their encouragement throughout the years kept me focused on the task at hand.

To Barry Neville, the editor now turned agent, who found me online and who called me to the plate after I spent a considerable time running around the outfield.

Building Wealth in a Paycheck-to-Paycheck World

1

Step 1: Drift and Conditions

Benjamin Franklin suggested once that the reward for a well-lived life was that you were useful, not rich. Too often we feel as though we would be better served by wealth. We yearn to be among those 13,000 tax-payers whose wealth is enviable. Their lifestyle is our golden ring.

I didn't know Sam when he taught history at Portland Community College. He loved those years as a teacher helping students get to the next level of higher education or simply relishing in the opportunity to enhance a student's outlook. He retired spending most of his time writing freelance articles about gardening and playing golf. He said that although he never did either, the stories he wrote about them kept him in "fun money." Sam is rare caricature, slightly bent over, muttering off-color jokes mostly for the amusement he gains from your discomfort. Sam is *the* consummate bond expert.

You have already met Kim. She is the single mom changing prices at the grocery store, waiting your tables, or brushing past you on a busy street on her way to some administrative assistant's job. She is a blue-collar every-woman. Always the hard worker, she often has felt like the working poor, living a life sometimes too close to the poverty line. She bought her first home about a year ago, was introduced to itemized taxes, and is thinking about doing something to finance her daughter's future.

As long as I have known him, Jorge has been planning some sort of escape. He has always dreamed of walking away from his job to do something else. He has tried his hand a planting Japanese maple trees, driving heavy machinery, and even running a country slaughterhouse. He has realized, despite his complaints about his current job, that he will always need

1

to work. He is at his happiest when he is employed. He doesn't drink, doesn't smoke, and doesn't otherwise waste his money. Even for all his self-reliance, he is distrustful of where he is in life, afraid that catastrophe waits around every corner. Jorge is an insurance agent's dream.

Jacob married a North African woman he met in California three years ago. The last time I spoke with him, he was waiting for the call to come home or to the hospital. The arrival of their first child was imminent, and he could hardly contain himself. By the time this book is published, he will be getting some up-close and personal lessons about fatherhood. At this stage in his life, he is the recipient of innumerable and mostly unsolicited pieces of advice, all of which he takes in good humor. He is a mutual fund collector.

And then there is Juli. She loves to shop. The trouble is doubled at her house largely because her husband shares the same passion to purchase what they cannot afford. Together they make every monetary mistake possible. They save nothing and consistently consume more than they earn. They have cars they cannot afford, live in a house larger than they need, and dress extremely well. He likes buying and collecting firearms; she sticks to lipsticks and purses.

None of the people I just mentioned is very much different from you. They are just a handful of the people you will meet in this book going through the cycles of work, play, family, vacations, and just going about this adventure we call life. Interrupting this, all too frequently, is money. It can be both financial pleasure and pain. As we follow single moms like Kim, young married couples like Jacob and his wife, and the rest of the everyday people I will introduce you to, remember one thing: It is incredibly easy to let your finances get away from you, take control, and become a burden rather than giving you a sense of freedom.

I understand that you may have come to this book looking for some "Holy Grail" of information that will somehow transform your existence, make you wealthy, and otherwise change your condition. You have come to the right place.

Inside these pages are more than just the tools you need, but the ability to understand your condition, change it, improve it, and make it more to your liking. Will you become as wealthy as those who live in that lofty 1 percent of the taxpayers as a result of reading this book? Quite possibly.

What I can't do is make predictions.

There is statistical research that shows how irrational we can be when it comes to money. Why do we purchase more insurance than we need? Why do we watch our portfolios take a headfirst dive into oblivion when we often have the information at our fingertips to stop our losses?

What you bring to this book are some preconceived notions about money. For some of you, money is urgent. It needs to be spent, moved, manipulated, or somehow transformed into the provider of creature comforts. For others, those creature comforts become the obsession that drives you to earn the money. For others, money is the biblical root of all evil.

Whoa, there, friend, you need to slow down and catch your breath. You need to understand that this process of building wealth is a slow, methodical one that is enhanced by time. It is a one-foot-in-front-of-the-other journey through a jungle of financial temptations and pitfalls. It is not as difficult a trip as you think it might be.

In the next nine chapters of this book we will deal with all the problematic issues that have stood in our way time after time. Together we will explore such things as risk and reward, how to prepare for the inevitable and the unexpected, and how much income you will need to get that done. We will explore a common problem called *style drift*. Style drift, as you will come to understand, is as much a part of our nature as pleasure and pain. If our ancestors had stuck with the same way of hunting and gathering, never expanding or rethinking their surroundings, those scruffy looking naked people running around 1.7 million years ago in the savannas mentioned in the Preface would have died out like so many mammal species before us. It was their ability to drift, or change, that was key to their survival. And it will be for you, too.

We are big-brained thinkers. Each and every one of us. We are impossible to predict. We are sensible and at the same time irrational. We are intelligent but find ourselves making poor financial decisions, time after time, even when the information seems readily available to help us, even save us. Many an economist has built his career around the concept that when it came to money, we would be logical, somehow predictable. In fact, however, we are a highly illogical group when it comes to how we spend and how we invest those hard-earned dollars.

This special grouping of individuals, numbering a couple hundred million, has earned the right to be called *blue class*. No more of this "white collar, blue collar" stuff. Instead, think of yourself as blue class. Taking the color out of the collar broadens the definition of who we think we are. We are workers. It doesn't matter what we do, whom we do it for, or how we earn that paycheck. If you need to work, you are blue class. If you need your paycheck, you are blue class. We are the majority who often act as if we were alone.

Some of us live a week-to-week existence with those checks. I want to change that. Many of us save too little and want too much. I think that we can change that. Many of you would like a house, perhaps even taking the next step toward investments, watching your money grow, and retiring to whatever dream you might have. I have some very good ideas to help you with all those items on your list. However, we need to begin at the most logical of places.

So sit back, kick your feet up, and pour yourself another cup of whatever it is you like to drink when you relax. This will take awhile. What do you say that we start with that stumbling block to any financial plan—debt?

2

STEP 2: Kick Your Debt

My youngest son Mike is taking a journalism class this year. As he talked one evening at the dinner table about the current day's writing activities, I turned the conversation in a different direction. I asked him what was his working definition for calling someone a victim. As a future journalist sent to cover a mishap, I asked, how would he determine who was and who wasn't a victim? I honestly thought there might be a difference in how people involved in accidents were defined.

I asked: "If someone goes into the water and drowns, would that person be considered a victim? If you get killed in a hurricane that you knew was coming, would you be a victim? If your car washes away in a flash flood on a road that was known for such occurrences, would you characterize yourself as 'victimized'?" He said yes, and understandably. The dictionary explains that victims are people who are at the mercy of a force or occurrence of nature.

I have always believed that a victim is someone who is caught unknowingly by some force, disqualifying anyone who actually, knowingly put himself or herself in harm's way from qualifying. For example, a surfer who gets bit by a shark is not a victim. Rest assured, the insurance people probably have a clearer definition.

Suppose, however, that those questions were turned toward money. Can a person who has experienced financial problems be considered a victim of debt? Could a person who buys a house that she could not afford be considered a victim of foreclosure?

Debt is often portrayed as some sort of weakness, a sort of financial disorder that is, unfortunately, shared by far too many people. Look around.

Whenever you are out and about, look closely at the faces in a crowd. You will be staring into the eyes of debt. For some, debt will rob them of their precious sleep. Others allow debt to creep in and disrupt their demeanor, making them angry or short-tempered. Many of us ignore it successfully, allowing it to creep about in the shadows, lurking behind the best financial intentions. For some, it is just the "American way," a fact of life, a given.

The majority of people in the blue class who carry debt do so wisely. They take their credit rating seriously. They pay any and all bills on time and in full. They may not understand how their diligence is helping everything from the cost of their insurance premiums to the interest rate on their mortgages. They will if they continue to read this chapter. They will understand how they have helped themselves to a financial treasure chest of savings unavailable to those who manage debt badly.

The rest of us who have failed to grasp the gravity of the situation and recklessly have found ourselves in over our heads cannot be called victims. A financial victim is taken unaware by some force of nature outside his control. This "natural" force is always economic. A loss of a job can make a person a financial victim. A medical bill beyond the scope of one's coverage can create financial havoc—that is, if you are fortunate enough to have coverage. Latest numbers published by the Kaiser Family Foundation put the number of Americans without any insurance at 43 million in 2002, and that number most assuredly is growing. These people are one step from becoming financial victims as well.

This is gloomy news indeed. The good news is that all is not lost. All it takes is a better understanding of the pros and cons, the uses and misuses, of debt to give us a solid footing on the long road ahead.

Brillig.com, a Web site that tracks the national debt as a way of reminding us that we are, indeed, a nation of debtors, recently showed that we the people of this great land owe a balance of $6,843,601,142,702.56. This phenomenal sum, until several years ago, actually was on the decline. Now each citizen's balance due is over $23,409.50. This is a difficult figure to comprehend.

In this chapter we will look at the nature of debt from the perspective of three types of debtors: the *reluctant debtor,* the person who is put in the position of accumulating debt because she needs to; the *recurring debtor,* which is what I call someone with good intentions but bad habits;

and the *political debtor,* who is a person who follows the lead of our government officials and spends as if he could print money.

There are several things all these debtors have in common. They lack a clear understanding of the negative effect that debt has on their future. As we look at these different types of people, I want you to keep in mind that there are numerous and justifiable reasons to go into debt. Some of them, such as buying a house, can be considered not only a necessity but also a kind of good debt. Finding the clear line between good and bad, necessary and unnecessary debt is what we will take a good look at in the following pages. It is an important second step.

THE POLITICAL DEBTOR

Harvard history professor Lizabeth Cohen recently wrote a lengthy study of what makes a consumer a consumer. According to her, we have been spending with wild abandon since the end of World War II and until recently have shown no signs of letting up. Her book, unfortunately, is a little over most of our heads, but the points she makes have a lot to do with the way we live. We are consumers, and as you will find, that comes with some real and tangible pressures.

After the terror attacks in New York and Washington, President Bush told Americans to get out there and keep spending. He acknowledged that we as consumers are the cornerstones of a prosperous economy. His plea to keep spending despite our reluctance to leave our homes was an effort to keep those dollars flowing. It was a noble effort. But the economy was slowing, and jobs were being lost before the attacks.

Let's stop here for a moment and look at the relationship of spending to debt. I want to talk about this so-called need of ours to spend. After World War II, a cycle began that created jobs that, in turn, created the ability to consume. The cycle is simple. It starts with a company producing a product, you purchasing it, and the company producing a replacement. The replacement product creates jobs, which provide paychecks for those who want to spend. This is capitalism at its finest. America had become a nation of consumers, and we are sitting in the driver's seat. Controlling two-thirds of economy can be a very powerful force for both consumers and the companies who cater to us.

The federal deficit, that huge number I mentioned earlier, growing at $1.5 billion a day, can have a negative influence on the way we think about debt. The federal government spends money. Once all the taxes—called *revenue,* by the way—are collected, the government pays its bills. If an adequate amount of tax is paid, then the budget, a laundry list of services provided for us, is balanced. This is much like at your house: If your paycheck matches all your expenses, your budget will be balanced. With this said, should the government run short of revenues but still need to spend, it borrows the money in the form of bonds.

Bonds, which we will discuss at greater length further on, basically work this way: Uncle Sam needs to borrow ten bucks, so he tells you he will give you 50 cents in interest for every $10 he borrows. Uncle Sam has always paid his debts before, so you lend him the money. Uncle Sam has a deficit. You, the bondholder, are the creditor. Like all debts, interest is charged. This is the 50 cents we charged him as the cost of borrowing.

Unfortunately, you can't issue bonds. However, your ability to repay a loan is worth something, much like Uncle Sam. This is called *creditworthiness.* No one lends to someone who is unable or unlikely to return the money. Creditworthiness is a heady compliment. This is where debts and deficits can get out of hand, often very quickly.

By the end of the last century, the government finally had a handle on its debts and was beginning to shown signs of a surplus. This created the possibility that Social Security might become fully funded just in time for the first wave of retiring baby boomers.

Juli is a political debtor. It took very little encouragement from her president to help justify her spending. She patriotically obliged. She bought an SUV, a hot tub, and redecorated her youngest child's room from paint to bedding—and never thought twice. Juli and her husband's income barely broke the $70,000 mark. But that didn't seem to matter. She was doing, in her words, her patriotic duty. Never before had being patriotic been so rewarding.

Juli and others like her believed that patriotism, however misguided, was achieved through the purchase of one consumer good after another. She told me that her president even explained the cycle of consumerism to her. Her country needed her.

The political debtor believes in the reason above all else. Using President Bush as an example of political debt is probably extreme. Presidents don't usually step up to the podium and encourage spending. Political debtors need a reason. They need only find a way to justify what they have bought.

Once you are able to justify the debt, the number associated with it—called *interest*—doesn't matter. It doesn't matter to Jacob that things lose value. The cost of the credit used to make these purchases continues to increase as the value decreases.

Consider this example of how debt costs work in reverse to the value: If you purchase a car for $30,000 at 6 percent interest, the true cost of that car is the purchase price plus the interest on the loan. This means that you will need to add $5797.44 to the purchase price. Disclosures mandated by the Truth in Lending Act will be given to you at the time the loan is signed so that you fully understand what you are spending. This is a good consumer law.

This is the true cost of debt. Depreciation drives down the value of the car as soon as you drive it off the lot. We all know that there is little likelihood that the car will be worth $35,797.44 at the end of the loan.

Political debtors can justify the services they purchase, the products they need, and the prices they pay. Political debtors tend to live for the "now" and worry little about the "later." As Professor Cohen writes: "Satisfying personal material wants actually served the national interest."

THE RELUCTANT DEBTOR

Behaviorists, those folks who study what we do and why, love the notion that we might get our ideas about debt from our parents or some other authority figure. These people, they contend, helped mold our ideas about money and debt. We followed their lead in many cases, for good and sometimes for bad. These people influenced the way we save or not, the way we spend, and the way we handle ourselves financially. These scientists found that our early examples of financial thinking can have a profound effect on us and the way we look at money.

For me, this lingering advice came from a ruddy-faced Irishman named John. John's financial outlook was simple: Find a career that people couldn't live without. For him, the choice involved two great depression era stalwarts, the butcher and the bartender.

The great depression was an economic disaster that influenced an entire generation's notion of money. Survivors of that period still try to explain how bad it can get. Baby boomers have struggled to keep such economic events far behind them and in so doing have forgotten some of the necessary lessons that can be learned from financial disasters. For the children of boomers, understanding money has become even further removed from the harsh realities of consequence. Without some great economic influence in our lives, we struggle with the concept of good times and bad. We develop financial half-truths that can stop our financial future from blossoming fully.

Debt can be a necessary, even useful part of life. Is it possible that debt can be both good and bad? Is there such a thing as good debt? Bad debt? Yes, yes, and yes.

Good debt can be for the purchase of a house. Bad debt can be for the purchase of the wrong house. Consider this: While a home for some would be a necessity, it may not be something you need. Broken down to its basics, a home is shelter. But a mortgage is quite another thing altogether. Later on I'll explain what this whole home-buying/mortgage thing is all about, but for now, we need to understand the relationship between your needs and the costs of those needs.

Let's start with the need for shelter. Folks who find themselves able to qualify for the purchase of a home should seriously weigh the pros and cons of tying their money up in a mortgage. This is an important problem at any age, but it should be considered seriously by first-time buyers. There is often a great deal of truth to the saying that "a home is a hole in the ground where you throw money." Few buyers are able to predict these costs accurately. If you can't determine these hidden expenses and are unable to budget for them, your home becomes the 800-pound gorilla in your financial world.

Affordable shelter, especially for those with tenuous finances, may mean renting. This is good for two reasons. It establishes a payment history and builds documents for both lenders and other types of creditors to reference in the future. And "throwing money away in rent" is not always as bad as the saying suggests. If renting allows you freedom in the form of mobility or cheaper commuting options or you simply aren't ready for the commitment of homeownership, then good for you.

Ideally, shelter provides a roof and four walls, protection from the elements, and a place to lay your head at night. A home comes with debt. A rental agreement comes with none.

Personally, I am all for homeownership. But what I am suggesting is that the right time is more important than the right house. The ability to determine whether the debt is good or bad or, even better, right or wrong for you comes with a good understanding of who you are. The better able you are to account for all the personal variables involved in such an enormous financial undertaking, the easier it will be to be comfortable with your decision. Buying a house you can't afford at too young an age can be an enormous financial and psychological setback. On the flip side of that same coin, renting for too long can make you lose focus and become complacent. Understanding the costs of each of these decisions almost demands that they should not be done in haste. Take your time, and do the math.

For older folks, those who don't consider themselves "as young as they used to be," a home can mean security, that is, equity. It can mean owning something they can fix, paint, landscape, and tinker with, as well as where they can plan a future. It is a place where they can spend a life. How many people do you know who are still in their "starter house" 20 and sometimes 30 years later? Many of us purchase a home with the intention of moving, but few of us get around to it. I've been in my first home for almost 20 years.

A house should be purchased when you can afford the debt and can continue to do so in the foreseeable future based on the income you earn. This is good debt. Often called the "American dream" and recently renamed the "American investment," your home can be a place of great value, solace, and comfort. This is debt worth having—as long as it is manageable.

Another example of good debt might be the purchase of appliances. Often referred to as *durable goods,* appliances are also considered a necessity. Good debt can be determined easily in two ways. One is *affordability.* Can you rest comfortably at night knowing that the income you earn is sufficient to cover your expenses? The other is *necessity.* Is it something that you, your partnership, or your family needs?

Always be a reluctant debtor. Be someone who is constantly questioning the need and the affordability of something before your eyes purchase what your wallet can ill afford.

THE RECURRING DEBTOR

Far and away this is the most common kind of debtor of the three. Unrestrained by reason and oblivious of the kind of debt, the recurring debtor is attracted to debt like a moth to a lamp. This is the debtor responsible for many of the following statistics. You probably have seen them:

Total consumer debt: $1.7 trillion—that's right, trillion with a *t*

Average debt carried by the average American: $8562

Total finance charges: $50 billion

The percentage of households in America deemed creditworthy by the lending industry: 78 percent

Number of credit-card holders declaring bankruptcy in 2002: 1.3 million

The recurring debtor is not alone, however. As I mentioned earlier, the economy depends on our ability to spend. Unfortunately, some people spend what they do not have. The next time you are sitting in traffic, look for the recurring debtor. The next time you are sitting in the lunchroom, look for the recurring debtor. The next time you are in the mall, look for the recurring debtor. Recurring debtors are easy to spot. They look just like us.

The economy has been playing directly into the psyche of these folks lately. Prices have dropped dramatically on many consumer goods as a result of a poorly performing or slowly recovering economy—depending on whom you talk to. These bargains, these rock-bottom prices, are hard to ignore. Retail prices on many goods are advertised as 50, 60, or 70 percent off, luring shoppers to save big money on items they probably were unaware they needed.

Reaching for your credit card to take advantage of these bargains would not happen if you had a solid financial plan in place. Successful financial plans need to have some sort of system of checks and balances, and this means that financial decisions should be made based on a partnership. It is a concept that is almost too simple.

Most of the problems faced by recurring debtors begin with impulse. The effect of that impulsiveness, a process that involves only you during the decision-making process, is full of problems. Creating some sort of system to help us distinguish the differences between what we need and what we want is very important. This means that you need a financial sounding board, someone who will listen, provide input, and be strong enough to make you think about the gravity of each financial decision you make.

If you are married or have a life partner, you need to have a full-blown discussion about your attitudes toward money, your financial outlook, and your experiences with credit. You need to do this from the beginning. If you haven't established an understanding before getting together, now is the time. You probably are already aware of each other's financial shortcomings. You will, mark my words, encounter debts throughout your relationship. There is no time better than now to discuss how you plan on approaching them—dealing with them.

If you are single, partnering with a parent, a best friend, or an older adult, preferably one who has had some experience with debt, should be considered. These people should act like a debt mentor. A good debt mentor helps you to look at your purchases and encourages you to stop and think before you buy that incredible "must have" item. They act like a financial sounding board, allowing you to discuss the pros and cons, as well as the consequences, on your current financial standing as well as future plans. You will not regret placing this financial hurdle in front of you.

In my case, this person, my voice of financial reason, is my wife, Bonni. As a child, her first lesson in understanding money came from watching the repo man take her father's car. She watched her household go from comfortable to poor and then back to comfortable. It was, as she has told me, incredibly difficult to comprehend as a child. As a result of these experiences, these early financial influences, she has a firm grip on every dollar in our household. She turned a poor financial beginning into a good financial journey.

Including someone like her in your life is an important step toward making sound financial decisions. You do not need to pay a financial advi-

sor for this help. It just needs to be someone who will listen and preferably someone who will tell you "I told you so" when you fail to listen to
them. Taking the time to find the right partner to help you discuss your
financial decisions is the key element in a healthy approach to debt.

THE SLIDING SCALE

Bad debt diminishes your ability to determine sensible financial goals for
yourself. Think about this for a moment. Debt, as we have discussed, puts
a negative pressure on any plan you may have in place or want to create.
Debt is simply the two steps backward for every one step forward.

At this point it is important to understand that debt can be fixed once
and for all. Two things are needed for this plan to succeed. The first is
help, and the second is the sliding scale. The help will be your financial
partner. First, put all your access to credit in a safe place, out of easy
reach. Then get all your credit bills in front of you.

The next step would be to list all your bills in order of smallest minimum payment to largest. For now, ignore the balances. We are concentrating on the minimum payments only.

In the example shown in the following figure, you will notice that
the four minimum payments, $27, $46, $65, and $88 are listed from least
to most.

Now for the sliding-scale magic. Double the payment for the smallest minimum by making a $54 payment instead ($27 + $27 = $54). At the
same time, continue to make the minimum payments on the remaining
bills.

The Sliding Scale

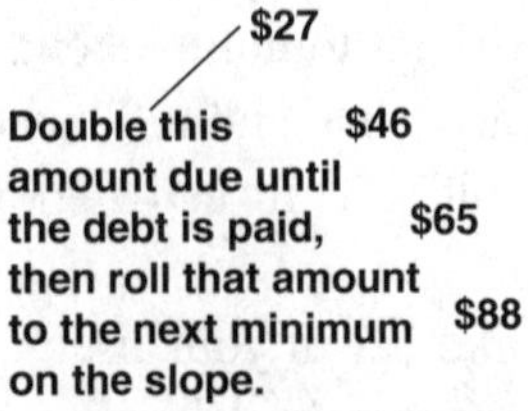

$27

Double this　　　$46
amount due until
the debt is paid,　　$65
then roll that amount
to the next minimum　$88
on the slope.

When you have paid off that bill, take that doubled minimum payment, in our example, $27 plus $27, and add that $54 to the minimum payment on the next debt, which is $46. Thus, instead of paying the minimum payment of $46, you are now making a $100 payment (see the following figure).

When that debt is paid in full, take the sum of that payment, now $100, and add that to the next debt ($65 + $100 = $165). These gradual increases, which still have not exceeded the original $27, eventually will eliminate your debt painlessly.

There are, of course, other ways to eliminate your debt, and I would be remiss if I didn't mention them. A popular method is called *snowballing* or *card hopping*. This is a credit-card game that involves switching balances for better interest payments in the short term. It buys time but does little to pay the debt if you aren't making any effort to pay more than the minimum on each card.

Often you will find yourself saddled with a credit card with high interest rates. A little comparison shopping will help you to find a card with a lower fixed rate, which translates into a lower minimum monthly payment. The lower minimum is not the concern here largely because you will be paying the minimum and then some. It is the interest that is accumulating while you pay the balance down that is important. You must understand that as you pay off these balances, interest is being charged on the money you owe. While you pay these cards off, you should help yourself to lower interest rates.

I mentioned the negative effect that debt can have on your financial goals. Here are some hard numbers: At Bankrate.com, the average rate for a 1-year certificate of deposit (CD) is around 1.58 percent at this writing.

The Sliding Scale

$0

$46 + $54

The doubled
payment now rolls to
the next debt
on the slope

$65

$88

The same site on the same day was posting credit-card weekly fixed averages of 12.98 percent. The difference between the savings and the debt is 11.40 percent. This is the cost of your debt.

So how do you get out of debt if you lack the discipline to use the sliding-scale method? There are several ways, none of which I recommend. Many of them involve borrowing, either from your personal savings or from another source, to pay the debt. Borrowing will not get you out of this mess but instead simply will spread out your existing debt over a longer period of time and land you a new creditor.

1. Borrowing against your life insurance can only be done on policies that have a cash value. As you will find out later in the book, the more expensive whole or universal life policies allow this kind of borrowing. Cash value usually is not associated with the less expensive term policies. You are, if you decide on this method, borrowing your own money; cash that will need to be repaid to the policy should you pass away before you have returned the money. Your beneficiaries will have the loan deducted from the amount of the policy if it hasn't been paid in full. The interest rates, though, are usually lower than those of most commercial lenders, especially when you factor in the cost of paper work. You cannot borrow more than the worth of the policy, so your beneficiaries won't be saddled with debt from this kind of borrowing. Think about it: Won't this be a fun way to be remembered—your policy less your debt?

2. Borrowing from friends and relatives is probably easier for some than others. I make it a rule to keep money out of relationships with family and friends. It keeps the relationship on better footing. Besides, you might need them for a real emergency and not just for bailing you out of your foolish spending habits.

3. Borrowing from your 401(k) or other retirement pension plan depends on the difference between your interest rate for your debt and the return on the investment. In recent years, many of the returns on these accounts have trailed the interest rates charged by many credit cards. Regardless of that, this is a patently bad idea. If you have debt, reduce or suspend temporarily any percentage or lump-sum contribution you are making to your retirement plan. Do this with one exception: If your employer is matching those contributions, reduce yours, whether it be a whole-dollar amount or a percentage, to the point where you can still get

the match, but no more. You will learn more about these kinds of plans later on, but that matching contribution is free money. Blue-class investors never turn their noses up at free money. When the debt is handled, resume your normal contribution.

4. Contacting your creditors either personally or through some sort of counseling agency will result in your credit report being updated with the information that you are participating in a debt management program (DMP). Using the DMP alternative avoids the longer-term (10 years) blemish that bankruptcy leaves on your credit report.

5. The temptation to make use of home equity to pay debts only extends the payments you have to make on your home. For many of us, our home is the best investment that we have. Tying your mistakes to your equity may prove unwise in the long run.

6. Bankruptcy, which is going to become harder under the Bush administration, is not really a viable option. It doesn't create the discipline you'll need to stay out of debt. It doesn't solve any of the problems with the way you were using your credit. I understand that there are often some serious reasons why a person would consider such a course. Loss of employment, poor health and the bills it creates, and other extenuating circumstances find people looking for relief from their bills. However, if all you did was spend more than you could repay, bankruptcy should be your last resort.

WHAT YOU CAN DO NOW

If you are carrying credit cards from multiple companies, try to consolidate them to a single card, preferably one with the lowest interest rate. If you have paid your bills on time and are currently in good standing, contact your credit-card company and ask for a better rate. It doesn't hurt to try. These companies know that your business is highly portable, so they may be open to your request.

Refinancing can reduce your monthly payments, freeing up additional cash that you can use to pay off other loans. Once again, I don't think it is smart to roll short-term debt into long-term mortgages by taking money out when you refinance. Lowering your monthly payment, however, is an excellent way to ease the burden and get those "ends" closer to meeting.

If you have a car loan that seems prohibitively high compared with what is now being advertised, perhaps you can refinance that as well. This is a newer type of refinancing, and lenders are limited to a few online sources at this writing, but it is possible that this could help with your monthly obligations.

DRAWING CONCLUSIONS

At the end of each chapter I will try to sum up what you have just read. In many of the following chapters you will be asked to go back to this chapter's conclusion and review it before moving on. This is how important this chapter is.

- If you are carrying debt, it has a negative effect on your financial plans. It is a subtraction of gains.
- When something loses value, it is called *depreciation.* It happens. Interest on a loan is now costing you more than the product's original value.
- Using any method to control your debt takes a committed person with a supportive partner. Sometimes both of you may need help. In that case, you should enlist a parent, ask a friend, or hire a counselor. There is nothing shameful about debt or asking for help.
- The sliding-scale method works incredibly efficiently but takes time and discipline. It builds character as well.
- If all else fails, find a free service to help. If you do, you need to understand several things. Nothing is really free. And if that is true, be cautious of what they are selling. If they offer to restructure your loans, sell you insurance, or have the perfect annuity for you, run for the door.
- Think about why you need to go into debt. If it is a vacation, a must-have toy, or even a remodeling of your home, the cost of the loan (the length of time and the interest rate) can greatly diminish the worth of the purchase. Try to plan some sort of advanced savings/payment plan (much like those quaint Christmas clubs the

local bank sponsors for kids), or take advantage of special free financing offers such as "12 months same as cash deals" or "zero interest for the life of the loan."

- Always read any paperwork associated with any type of loan arrangement. Pay close attention to penalties for prepayment or delinquency and any conditions that need to be followed.

3

Step 3: Take Responsibility for Your Money

James Burke, host of the popular television program, "Connections," once pointed out, as he so often did, that many of the factors that lead to discoveries and inventions were interconnected, unpredictable, and often accidental. Often he found that the storyline of his show was "more like the path of a pinball caroming about its table than a linear chain of events." This "pinball effect," if I might borrow from Mr. Burke for a moment, quite possibly resembles the state of your finances and your understanding of them. Budgets turn your financial world into a linear chain of events, forcing your money in the right direction.

The problem is simple: When it comes to our finances, many of us have received a string of mixed messages that come at us from every angle. We are inundated with commercials encouraging us to buy now, pay later. We hear about no-hassle credit cards and deferred payments. There are countless ads offering us expensive automobiles with nothing down, no interest, and in some cases no payments for several months. Credit-card approvals arrive in the mail even to those who have declared bankruptcy. And even after the terrorist attacks of September 11, 2001, the president spoke to the people and in the process of emphasizing economic strength made spending sound like some sort of patriotic duty.

Few of us think first about this simple fact: Spending always comes with consequences. In Chapter 2 I mentioned a partnership with someone you can use as a financial sounding board. In this chapter I want to talk more about the role of that partnership in a healthy financial relationship.

THE BEST LAID PLANS

Leland has a budget. Tim offered his version when I told him I was writing this book. And Juli has a budget too. When I asked her how her budget worked, she responded, "Well, we sort of, kind of, well, we know how much we can spend each week."

The budgets that people show to me don't differ much from one another. The basics of a budget, at least a good one, are designed to guide you in your life, keeping you within the confines of your paycheck. It almost sounds too simple.

Leland's budget, like so many, is a simple plan needing only two elements: discipline and desire. He explained the particulars of his budget and how it worked to a young coworker. This kid would be broke by the end of the week, he told me. Standing in a grocery store parking lot, he explained the plan. The young man would write "Week 1," "Week 2," "Week 3," and "Week 4" on four separate envelops. Into these he would place his monthly expenses divided by four. If the rent payment was $400, he would place $100 in the envelope marked "Week 1." If his utilities cost $100 a month, he would put $25 away. With each paycheck, the process would be repeated. This simple system worked for the kid, Leland told me. After filling the envelops with the necessary payments, the young man knew what was left to spend.

Tim's budget came with paperwork, was more detailed, and the sheet encompassed a far more complicated financial situation. Every imaginable expense was listed. Those expenses were subtracted against a four-paycheck month. His simplistic 48-week system rewarded the good budget with a bonus paycheck. With 52 weeks in a year, Tim's budget allowed a fifth (weekly) paycheck four times a year. In 2003, this bonus check would have kicked in January, April, August, and October.

This budget requires some sort of financial fresh start, a windfall of cash that let's you begin all over again. Should that happen to you, this is a good way to keep your finances under control. Stripped to its core, Tim's budget is like Leland's: It requires discipline and desire.

Juli's budget is probably far more representative of most people's budgets in America today. It is a haphazard and loosely formed plan that relies on dividing major bills, such as the house payment, insurance costs, and payments for both cars, and having them deducted electronically and paid by her bank. Whatever is left covers food and miscellaneous expenses such as entertainment and clothing. This sort of passive budgeting is, on the surface, better than none at all.

THE INVESTMENT PLAN

- Place a priority on debt reduction, starting with credit cards using a sliding scale (see Chapter 2).
- Identify upcoming expenses with the house, estimating the costs of possible major repairs, and start an allowance account to cover quarterly, semiannual, and annual obligations such as taxes and insurances.
- Evaluate spending on the family, such as vacations, school expenses, and braces for the kids.
- Develop a solid retirement plan that is both reasonable and attainable.

One of the first things you and your financial partner need to do is define what it is you plan on doing for the year. All you need to do is determine what day that will be. Businesses call this the *beginning of their fiscal year.* They call the plan a *financial forecast.*

This plan should answer such questions as: Is this the year I paint the house? Am I going to need to replace any major appliances? Do I plan a vacation? Are the kids going to need braces? Special schooling? Camps? Sporting events? Entertainment? What financial difficulties might pop up in the upcoming year?

You probably will be surprised at the your answers. Juli has admitted to me that her toughest question doesn't start with "Can we afford?" but rather with "How can we afford?" The differences are subtle, and the answers are vital to the success of your plan.

A good budget understands what will be asked of it. A good budget takes the consequences of all your financial decisions into consideration.

Life is full of unexpected emergencies. These monetary bumps should not break a budget, but your budget should allow you to better absorb them. Budgets provide financial resiliency that would not exist without them.

Your Budget Projections: Now to a Year from Now

Budget Income Year	Budget House Year	Budget Taxes Year	Budget Insurance Year	Budget Debt Year	Budget divided by 13
$50,000					$3846
	$12,000				− 923
		$2,500			− 192
			$4,800		− 369
				$6,000	− 461

Juli and her husband's financial difficulties are based on a poor but widely practiced notion called *division of incoming revenue.* This is kind of a fancy term for what's mine is mine, what's left over is ours. The simplest solution to this problem starts with this concept: In a financial partnership, your paycheck is your contribution—every dime of it.

I am always amazed by couples that keep money separate from their mutual budget. If you have entered into a financial union (and every marriage is a legal and binding contract), why would someone undermine the integrity of that agreement by stashing money outside the budget. If you are single, the financial agreement is with your partner who oversees your budget's success. Every dime counts toward the goals you may have set, the hopes that the budget will fulfill, and the future that the budget will fund. Do not shortchange your plan.

Next, list all your expenditures. An *expenditure* is basically a bill, a debt, or an obligation. This can be a loan, a car payment, or child support. Each item lays bare your financial past and present. These all play a role in shaping your financial future. If these total less than you earn, the result is called a *surplus.* Hooray! Your budget will begin to work its way toward your future faster. If your bills, debts, and obligations are more than what you earn, you have a *deficit.*

A *deficit* is, by definition, "an excess of expenditure over revenue." This is a problem that you may not have understood fully prior to this. It can be an eye-opener indeed.

After this is done, close the book and walk away—together. It is time to discuss what you have just done. It can be overwhelming. You have brought to the table, for the first time in one place, your whole financial present, as well as your financial past.

Set up another time, preferably within the next day or so, and sit down and move on to the next step. The next step redefines your partnership or sole proprietorship in business terms.

Your "annual budget meeting," as it is now called, has a beginning—a starting point that runs either a surplus or a deficit. Now it is time to forecast for the future—much the same way a business does.

After you have added all your income revenue and totaled it, divide the number by 13. For instance, $50,000 total household income divided by 13 equals $3846. This is the figure you will use to express your budget in terms of income. Why 13? This number is often used by corporations to even out the year into equal parts. Fifty-two weeks divided by 13 equals 4 weeks.

Unfortunately, your obligations may or may not follow this schedule. This is where it gets complicated. To simplify this as much as possible, think of it this way: Your fiscal year starts on April 1, for example. Your house payment in due on the fifteenth of each month. On a 13-month calendar, the fifteenth actually moves. The next fiscal month begins on April 29, 28 days later, or 4 weeks. The fifteenth of the month is now magically moved to May 13. The next fiscal month, 28 days after April 29, begins on May 26. By June 10, you have enough earned to pay a house payment that normally was due 5 days later. July 8, August 5, and so on.

In the example at the beginning of this section, the figures assume that your income taxes are paid in full from your paycheck but do not include your property taxes. The insurance figure (only an example) may not even be close to what you are paying for property, automotive, and health insurance. The credit-card payment is based on an even split of the balance by 13 months, excluding any interest.

Once your obligations have been accounted for in this manner, it is somewhat easier to see what is left over. Hopefully, this number reflects a surplus. I say hopefully because we haven't even accounted for food, clothing, incidentals for work, and the kids.

Many popular economists say that government runs best when it runs a deficit. Those same people also feel that if the government is running surpluses (bringing in more money than it needs), then we are being taxed too much.

You, on the other hand, are not permitted to run your little household/business with deficit spending. You need surpluses and a steady stream of month-after-month profits. And to do that, you need to identify your expenditures, recognize current deficits, predict your future ones, and adjust your family's spending habits.

THE RULES

There was a time when debt was simple. You either had credit or you didn't. Credit was difficult to come by. For big purchases, you had to save, scrimp, and do without to save enough money to get what you wanted. Now all you need to do is throw down a little piece of plastic, sign on the dotted line, and you are out the door with whatever your heart desires.

This so-called freedom is why you need rules—or maybe not rules so much as guidelines.

Rule Number One

- *It will take longer than you assume to create a working budget.*

Necessity is the first reason to approach a budget. As much as we look forward to growing up and reveling in all those freedoms that grownups have, we often neglect to factor in the costs associated with those perks. We all have friends with hot cars, nice clothes, and a party lifestyle. We all have acquaintances that seem to live large while we struggle to get by. It is easy to become envious of their good fortune.

Mark Twain once said, "The lack of money is the root of all evil." He also said, "You can't reach old age by another man's road." These are good quotes about lack of money and the cost of envy. Understanding that the Jones's are broke is a monumental breakthrough in financial thinking. As American consumers, we are inundated with offers and products. There is no escape from the parade of pleasures available to us. The first challenge to your budget will be ignoring those temptations. Some of you already know how quickly you can bring down your financial house once you allow yourself to succumb. It takes very little time to go from having money (a surplus) to being totally broke to being in debt (a deficit).

Rule Number Two

- *You can do this. It is only a matter of perspective.*

This whole idea of budgeting is a lot easier if you understand a few simple things. Money, as you know, is something you earn. But few of us break down the everyday cost of the things we buy against our paychecks. Is a $12 haircut different from a $30 one? Based on the average hourly wage in this country, the answer is yes. With an average hourly wage of $15.48 in America, based on a number generated by the Bureau of Labor Statistics from September 2003, you don't even need a calculator to see the impact of something as minor as a haircut on an hour worked. Our understanding of the direct relationship between the twenty bucks you just handed your teenage child and the time it took to earn it is usually the farthest thing from our minds—and theirs.

Rule number two breaks down this way: The more you understand about how you earn money, the more you are likely to be slower to part with it. This change of perspective is a sudden revelation for most people. Once you can comprehend the relationship between your expenses and how long it took you to earn the money to pay for them, you will be ready for the gradual acceptance that you can break your free-spending habits.

So far we have done what a financial planner would have done. We started with a little information gathering. We know how much money comes in and how much is going out. Now we will put it on paper.

---

    1. Gross monthly income, average (total yearly ÷ 13)   _____

Payroll deductions:

    2. Taxes (federal, state, local)   _____
    3. Savings plan (401k, 403b, credit union)   _____
    4. Other (medical, dental, etc.)   _____
        Total payroll deductions
        Net income (gross minus deductions)   _____

Expenses:

    5. Personal savings (pay yourselves first)
    6. Housing (rent or mortgage)   _____

Continued

7. Utilities	_____
8. Home maintenance (laundry, toiletries, upkeep)	_____
9. Transportation (purchase, lease, or public)	_____
10. Auto upkeep (gas, insurance, license, etc.)	_____
11. Food (groceries, dining out)	_____
12. Clothes	_____
13. Books, periodicals, online services	_____
14. Entertainment (TV, movies, CDs, vacation)	_____
15. Debt (credit cards, school, etc.)	_____
16. Other expenses	_____
Total expenses	_____
17. Income, net minus all expenses	_____

Monthly Budget

Herbert Hoover once said that, "the course of unbalanced budgets is the road to ruin." The following little chart will keep that from happening.

Line One: Gross Monthly Income

1. Gross monthly income, average (total yearly ÷ 13)	_____

In the first part of our budget, we need to tally the entire household's income in what is called *gross form*. Gross income is what you earn before taxes and any other deduction you may have set up. Earlier in this section I suggested that you divide the year into 13 parts. Each of these parts represents your monthly gross income, which together represent your yearly gross income. Ask someone how much he earns, and this is usually the figure he tells you.

Remember to be honest with yourself here. If you can count on certain yearly bonuses, alimony or child support payments, or other regular payments that the Internal Revenue Service (IRS) may be interested in, your budget will be interested also. If scheduled raises due to some sort of evaluation or union contract are part of your income year, include them also.

Child support, alimony, and trust payments should be added in as well. Some budgets suggest that you build in a cushion by using the smallest amount of income possible. This is a bad idea. It creates a false monthly surplus that is mistaken as free money and eventually leads to frivolous spending.

Lines 2 through 4

Everybody wants his or her piece of your money pie. Once you have determined your gross income, remove your tax obligations, and enter them on line 2. There are federal, sometimes state, and sometimes local taxes that occur on a regular basis. One of the best guides is the tax return you filed last year. You will find the best approximation of what your tax bill will be for this year in last year's numbers.

While we are on the subject of taxes, make sure that your monthly deductions match what you actually owe. March yourself into your payroll or human resources office and change your deductible until you come as close to zero taxes owed on April 15 as possible.

I want to take a minute to share a pet peeve. Every year I hear about folks who can't wait to file their taxes to get the refund they have coming. They have earmarked this overpaid tax money for any number of things from a vacation to paying off Christmas bills to simply splurging on some sort of shopping spree. People like Juli, Jacob, and friends too numerous to list barely get to the end of the month financially. Yet every year they rush to their friendly tax preparer, file electronically, pay extra for the speed, and then take the money and run. I know one guy who even uses his father's tax preparation service. In complete disregard of his dad's advice, he will pay dear old Uncle Sam extra money all year long. I know some people who receive as much as $2000 back. Every year. That's $38 a week that could have been saved, earned interest, been invested, or otherwise have been used to help keep you out of debt. Don't overpay, and even more important, don't *underpay*. Use the W-4 form in your employer's office to calculate exactly the right amount of deductions needed to come out as close to zero owed, zero returned.

Using your pay stub, you can determine the approximate amount of money you paid to Social Security, disability, and Medicare.

As we go through this book, there will be other mentions of taxes and their implications in your attempt to build wealth. What we are trying to build is a base of financial knowledge. It will change, but at least you will have a starting point.

Income Deductions

Payroll deductions:

2. Taxes (federal, state, local)   _____
3. Savings plan (401k, 403b, credit union) _____
4. Other (medical, dental, etc.)   _____

Total payroll deductions   _____

Later, when we get to investments in Chapter 9, I will spend some serious time discussing your savings plan, specifically your 401(k), your IRAs, and any other type of pension. There are pros and cons in this type of investment that you will need to know. For now, use line 3 for the amount you contribute into your employer-sponsored benefit plan. If you are saving in any other pretax or after-tax plan, include this figure here.

Line 4 depends on your employer's health care plan. You may have some weekly dollar amount taken out to pay your premium. If so, enter that number. Better yet, be realistic and increase it by 15 percent.

Income Minus Deductions

Net income (gross minus deductions)   _____

At this point you can take a look at your financial picture with a somewhat clearer eye. Now, for the expenses. Unfortunately, no matter how you try to master your personal finances, you will always have expenses.

Expenses

Expenses:

    5. Personal savings (pay yourselves first)   _____

    6. Housing (rent or mortgage)   _____

    7. Utilities   _____

    8. Home maintenance (laundry, toiletries, upkeep)   _____

    9. Transportation (purchase, lease, or public)   _____

   10. Auto upkeep (gas, insurance, license, etc.)   _____

   11. Food (groceries, dining out)   _____

   12. Clothes   _____

   13. Books, periodicals, online services   _____

   14. Entertainment (TV, movies, CDs, vacation)   _____

   15. Debt (credit cards, school, etc.)   _____

   16. Other expenses   _____

Total expenses   _____

The primary question here is, Can you be realistic in estimating these costs? These numbers are the first step in creating a reliable budget. Believe me when I tell you that this is the one section of the budget that is totally in your control.

Line 5 is the second time in the budget where savings are mentioned. This isn't accidental. Savings should be thought of as an expense. It is taken directly from money left after taxes. The old saying, "Pay yourself first," is and always will be an excellent idea. Finding the right amount to pay yourself can be difficult if you have never done it. If your savings plan is too aggressive—if you are paying yourself too much— you may find yourself more likely to assume some debt. This is never a good idea, even in the short term. Remember in Chapter 2 we discussed the negative effects that debt causes to savings. Debt costs money. You will need to adjust your goals by reducing your deductions. So save. It is important.

Lines 6 through 16 are the workable parts of a good budget. These are the parts of a budget that can be adjusted. These figures are less fixed and far more flexible. Taking a long, hard look at these expenses can lead to some additional savings that you may have been known existed.

These "workable" parts of the budget can be achieved by some common sense and good, old-fashioned penny pinching. For instance, do you leave the heat on when you aren't home? Are there ways to curb your utility bills? Does the two-car garage need two cars in it? Can you really justify the added costs of upkeep, insurance, and gas?

How often do you eat out? Is it because you can't cook or because you don't want to? When you shop for food at the grocery store, are name brands always better than store brands? Do you shop for clothes because they are simply on sale? Do you read all the magazines and newspapers you subscribe to? Do you buy books and never get around to reading them (not including the book you are holding, of course)? Do you avail yourself of online services that you don't need?

I think you get the drift of this. These questions need to be asked. Financial common sense begins with a series of questions just like the ones I just asked. They are meant to help us understand that wanting and needing are two entirely different things.

Rule Number Three

- *Stay with your plan.*

You have considered a budget for a reason. Perhaps it is more than just finding a few extra bucks at the end of the month. Maybe your goals are loftier. Maybe you want to buy a home or pay off the one you own. It is important to know exactly where you stand financially before you start chasing your dreams.

Now, for the real reason we use budgets. It is not because I want to see you calculate where you are or where you've been. I want you to determine, based on your budget, where you are going. In the past, you had no difficulty identifying what you wanted. Impulses are short-term goals. Budgets create the ability to achieve long-term goals.

Budgets make you think about what it is that you want. Is it a house? Is all you can think about those lazy afternoons watching the kids play on the front lawn while you sip something that makes the glass sweat? Perhaps it is tinkering in the garage or working in the garden. Budgets are the only tool that will get you there.

Accountability, or honesty, in your budget is extremely important. You do not want to exclude some of those guilty pleasures that make life worthwhile. If you can't live without that $5 coffee in the morning, budget for it. If you want to see a movie every Saturday or rent one or two for the weekend, budget for it. Too many people are missing the point when they begin a budget. You are different from everyone else. You have different needs and wants, different goals and ambitions, and different abilities and willpower. Your budget should reflect this individuality.

DRAWING CONCLUSIONS

If you haven't read Chapter 2, please go back and do so now. Controlling debt is essential to any good budget.

- The heart and soul of every good budget contains three basic elements: discipline, desire, and honesty.
- A good budget is a financial plan that helps you to attain both short- and long-term goals. Budgets create monetary discipline, good savings habits, and a deeper understanding of how your personal finances work.

4

Step 4: Invest Where You Hang Your Hat

I can't stress enough the value of the three preceding chapters—you know, the ones you perused, glanced over, or otherwise skipped altogether. This book is built on individual steps in a wage earner's life. You may be laboring under the belief that once you own your home, have a 401(k) plan at work, and are fairly far along on life's road, you probably have done so without a good financial foundation. That, I'm afraid, cannot be started from the middle. The only thing that can happen from that particular point is change. With change comes understanding. With understanding comes knowledge, and although I did not say it first, with knowledge comes power. Change is the only thing you can do from the middle. From the middle of a bad plan, you can change the course you are taking.

That said, you really should have good understanding of how to think about money, how to devise a plan for the second essential need of life (after air), and how to manage it. Over the course of 5 or 6 months, Kim, our working blue-class single mom I introduced to you in Chapter 1, and I had numerous conversations, none more than 5 minutes long. They were all about what we discussed here in the first three chapters. She wanted a house. And more important, she wanted to keep it.

So go back and review those first three chapters so that we all are on the same page.

As long as I have known Kim, she has had as vibrant a personality as the deep red color of her hair. She is driven, with a "take no prisoners" attitude. She knows what she wants, and when she sets her mind to the goal, she never loses sight of it. When Kim told me that she had made the decision to buy a home, her signature on the loan papers was as sure as rain in the Northwest part of this country.

Somewhere along the line, Kim developed and nurtured a dream that involves owning something that she could call her own. As we talked over those months, I realized that this complicated process frequently is not even totally understood by those who already own homes. Those folks probably will stumble through a refinance with little more than passing knowledge of the process, and this is not good. There is a lot of money at stake here, and such a situation deserves your undivided attention. Each home-buying experience is different, with its own set of circumstances, terms, and participants.

The latest Census numbers report that there are 72,265,000 owner-occupied homes in this country. If you are in one of those homes, great! In this chapter I will familiarize you with your loan and prepare you for refinancing if the opportunity presents itself. If you don't own a home, this chapter will unlock many of the mysteries of buying a home, from acquiring and understanding your credit to examining your motives.

YOUR CORNER OF THE WORLD

Homeownership can be broken down into two basic components, buying and selling. The complications involved in these two simple words and the decision to jump into this life-altering situation make home buying one of the most rewarding and frustrating exercises in finance many of us will ever undertake.

When I was newly married, I had no idea that I wanted a home. Many young people, at least in their younger, more formative years, are less interested in such matters. They feel more transient and free without a house. Reluctantly, a few of my friends have purchased a home as a way of avoiding unnecessary contributions to the federal tax reserves. (There are some serious tax advantages to owning a home that I will discuss at length later.) They understood after years of contributing to their landlords' coffers that they could own a place of their own. But these people are in the minority. It isn't until we take on a financial partner, in my case my wife Bonni, that we understand the meaning of "a house is a necessity."

Homeownership is a very attractive option for many people. Both women and men, single or together, need to be able to call someplace home. Not just a house, but walls that can be painted, rooms that can be personalized, and perhaps gardens that can be tended to on sunny days. They see a storybook yard to fill with kids, toys, and pets. Perhaps a house located in a neighborhood where people talk over the fence, wash their cars on Saturday afternoons, and play basketball in the streets

Often, both domestic and nondomestic types alike discover, sometimes by surprise, that this necessity will have faults. It will always need to be repaired, I'm sorry to say, forcing many a novice to learn which end of a hammer is for business. Homeowners will learn how to read instructions, memorize silly screwdriver rhymes such as, "righty-tighty, lefty-loosey," and learn how to repair a toilet. You will find yourself in some huge home repair superstore looking for bonding compound, screen doors, wallpaper, or screws.

With any good fortune, those instructions will be on how to build a swing set. With any good fortune, you will find yourself running your child down the sidewalk, hand on the seat, teaching her the fine art of bike riding. You will throw footballs in the nearby park and barbecue in the back yard on sultry summer nights. And you will find yourself rocking on the front porch 50 years later realizing that these memories were all made possible by the simple purchase of a house.

It is this notion of peace and calmness that hooks you and makes all the aggravation, the sleepless nights, and the scrimping together of those nickels and dimes worth it.

There are steps involved in this process, and the first is self-discovery. However, self-discovery involves more than saying, "I want a house!" Although it is often reduced to that as a jumping off point, there is a certain amount of soul searching that is often ignored in the quest for homeownership. The first questions should be, "Can I buy a house of my own?" and "Should I buy one?"

Let's talk about whether you can purchase one first. Your debt, which we covered at length in preceding chapters, from this point forward will be termed your *debt ratio* by those fine folks in the lending business. This is the amount of money you owe compared with the amount of money you make. The amount you earn we'll call *assets*. The acceptable level of debt expressed as a ratio can vary widely from lender to lender. If your debt is in control, this will be used as a yardstick to measure your worthiness, or your ability to pay a monthly mortgage payment on time every month for the next 30 years or so. This is sort of a qualifying round.

Once you make the decision to step up and ask for an enormous sum of money to purchase a house, there are certain criteria the lender requires you to meet. One of the most important is a job. Kim has one that provides her and her 5-year-old with a comfortable living but not very many luxuries. One of the first lessons she learned was one of the hardest.

Having a good debt ratio is not the same as good credit. Remember debt ratio is the difference between what you earn and what you owe. This is expressed as a percentage. Using 40 percent as the ceiling, the lower the percentage of debt to income, the better it is in terms of interest rate. Credit, on the other hand, is your ability to borrow money and repay that money with interest according to the terms of the loan.

Lenders like folks who work. Lenders like to see regular paychecks from dependable earners. To them, dependable workers translate into good risks. Giving money to people is always a risky affair, and lenders like to limit those risks as much as possible.

The combination of income, debt ratio, and credit history plays an important role in determining the amount of money you qualify for, the type of loan you may receive, and the interest rate. For the lender, these all add up to risk.

Lenders lend money to make money. Risk is something they are willing to take but are reluctant to do without compensation. Risk is reduced by a steady income, few obligations, and a good credit score. You are rewarded with better terms on your loan. Lenders have little interest in your dreams. They have little interest in your plans once you have the house. Their interest begins and ends with the money involved and your ability to pay it back in full with interest month after month. They try to paint a sunnier picture of the process, but essentially this is what it is all about—risk.

It is important to note that the amount of income you are receiving actually has increased at a slower pace than the cost of housing in this country. It has been reported recently that the median family income grew by only 10 percent over the last 20 years or so, but during the same time, housing prices have increased in value as much as 300 percent in some places.

This little piece of fair warning leads to this: The home of your dreams may not be exactly the building you can afford. It might contain less in total square footage or be located in a neighborhood that is different from the one you probably imagined. Kim found this little dose of reality the only downside in the whole process.

She instead chose to concentrate on the upside and a much brighter prospect: These lenders wanted to lend her money.

Lenders will do their best to get you into the right loan based on your income. It is how they make their living. They really want to make sure that your loan is just right for you.

The simplest rule when it comes to borrowing money for a home is: The higher the income in relation to the debt, the better the loan you are likely to get. The rhyme is purely coincidental, but the fact is plain and often comes as a surprise to first-time home buyers. It doesn't mean that you need a lot of income. It simply means that the difference between what you take home and what you owe to your creditors should be separated by as wide a margin as possible. The ability to manage money and, specifically, your debt is very important.

YOUR REPORT CARD

While some people will suggest that determining how much house you can afford should be the first step, it does little toward getting you into a loan. In fact, buying a home is all about the quality of your debt, and this will determine the quality of your loan.

The grim reality of every loan you apply for, no matter what it is you are buying, is based on reports generated by your previous creditors. Those previous creditors or lenders have given you a grade based on how you handled your loan. Much like those report cards from school, those grades are part of a permanent record lenders can reference time and time again with every loan application. This report contains a detailed list of money that was loaned to you, the length of the loan, and how you handled it (paid it back).

This report is produced by credit agencies for lenders, and it shows every account that involves credit issued in your name. Every gas card, department store charge account, furniture loan, and auto purchase agreement are listed. I think that you will agree that this is pretty important stuff. It is advisable to check this report every year or two. Beyond that, it becomes difficult to correct mistakes—and lenders *do* make mistakes in reporting. If you have had some credit activity (paid off a loan or closed an account), it is a good idea to check periodically to make sure that these transactions have been recorded properly.

But wait; there is more than just this open and closed account information on your report. Beneath this veneer of information is a decipherable pattern. This report contains a tapestry of financial transactions and is a history that is yours alone. Below the surface, under the numbers, lies the real report card. Your FICO score.

Fair, Isaac and Company, or FICO, is a credit research company that creates this underlying score. Since the inception of the FICO scoring system, this California company has become the major source that lenders and insurers use to determine your creditworthiness. For a mortgage lender, your FICO score has become a key factor in determining the amount of your monthly payment. Recently, insurers also have begun to use this system. For an insurance company, this FICO score may determine the amount of your premium or the coverage you can buy.

The method by which FICO arrives at your score is still a well-guarded secret, but that veil is slowly coming down. There are, however, certain things we can learn from our score. As an applicant, your score can save or cost you a great deal of money over the long haul. There is a direct relationship between the quality of your credit and the interest rate you receive. The better the score, the lower is the rate. Although other things factor into your ultimate interest rate, credit has the biggest and most costly impact. Something as simple as an interest rate a half a point higher can mean thousands of dollars over the length of the loan.

FICO does have guidelines for the consumer to follow if you want to improve your score, and the guidelines are based mostly on good credit sense. The score is broken down into several categories:

- *Payment history.* What is your track record? Your payment history accounts for up to 70 percent of your total score. Late payments aren't necessarily considered "score killers" according to the FICO Web site, but then again, neither is paying everything off each month able to net you a perfect score. FICO is quick to point out that good credit histories help in your overall score. This category takes into account late payments (60 days late is better than 90 days late), bankruptcies, foreclosures, lawsuits, wage attachments, liens and judgments, types of accounts, install-ment loans, and the satisfaction of any judgments against you.

- *Amounts owed.* How much is too much? Of course, the best advice here is to make sure that your payments to any loans or debt are made on time. FICO gives no indication of how a perfect score is achieved in this category, but definitely, good common sense with creditors will help you score higher. If you are having credit difficulties such as late or missed payments, you need to resolve these issues prior to applying for a home loan. The same advice applies if you are looking to purchase an insurance policy. With the average balance on consumer credit cards hitting the $11,000 mark, it is always good advice to keep those balances as low as possible. The scorekeepers also like to see consistency in payments. One-time paydowns or lump-sum payments don't have much of an effect on your overall score.

- *Length of credit history.* How established is yours? You are graded on your ability to get credit and pay it down. This will provide a higher score than paying off credit cards in full each month. Odd as that sounds, it is your skill at managing debt from month to month, not your use of credit as a sort of convenience, that inter-ests the FICO scorekeepers. Any balance owed is taken into con-sideration, as well as how much credit is available and whether you have used it all. It seems that the best method to score higher in this category, which is worth 30 percent of your total, is to maintain no more than three credit cards with low balances (and regular payments made to those balances). Too many credit cards will lower scores.

Beware of the balance game. This popular game involving shifting balances from one card to another will come back to haunt you when you are scored in this category. While the balance game is at it's core an attempt to get low introductory rates on another card, it leaves too many cards open for scrutiny. Shop around for the best deal, and stick with it.

- *Types of credit use.* Is it a "healthy" mix? Credit history is all about your ability to manage your finances or, in this case, loaned money. This category nets a 15 percent share of your total score based on a healthy mix of loans. Beginners will open every account that is thrown their way. Save some percentage from your purchase if you open an account is often offered at department stores and other retailers. Unwittingly and before you realize it, you have far too many accounts open. FICO considers this too much available credit. Live within your means, and keep your accounts to a minimum.

- *New credit.* Are you taking on more debt? It is almost impossible to avoid the offer of credit. Some of us will ruin our credit in college long before we even have a chance to establish any real money management skills. If you are just starting out, be careful. The FICO people are looking for a little caution, perhaps a small amount of financial maturity at this stage. Poor scores in this category are more a result of too much too soon. Establishing credit is good. Taking every offer that comes your way is bad.

Each time you apply for a credit card or a loan or otherwise engage in a transaction where money is being lent, a report is generated. Each of these reports can have a negative effect on your overall score. Keep in mind that checking your own credit report, which is something you should do periodically, especially in these times of identity theft, is not scored against you. If you have applied for a loan and are shopping around, try to make your decision within a month. There is a time-frame issue with the scorer.

So what is the best score? Well, 720 is considered average, and it can move in either direction depending on what you have done credit-wise. For instance, paying your bills on time will be considered for almost 70 percent of your score and will get your score to 727. This might be a good time to set up some sort of automatic payment system to keep yourself punctual.

Here are some things to remember: The difference between a credit score and a credit report is significant. A *credit score* is a snapshot of how you use your credit, whereas a *credit report* merely details activity. While the two are intertwined, the credit report is more comprehensive, looking at open accounts, balances, payments, liens or bankruptcies, and any other public information that the lender considers important. In order to have a sterling report or get yourself to that state, you need to check it for discrepancies as often as every 2 years. Paying your bills on time, keeping your accounts clean and the balances low on as few accounts as possible, and striving to be financially neat and normal are essential.

Suppose that your report is less than stellar. The fix is easy but will, as in all things involving money, take time. The first thing to do is to look at the reported personal information. A gaff in something as simple as a Social Security Number can lead to bad reporting. Criminal convictions will stay on your credit report indefinitely. Bankruptcies stay on the report for 10 years, whereas missing or late payments to a creditor, according to the Federal Consumer Information Center, linger on the report for 7 years.

In order to fix those problems, compare all the available reports side by side. Make a determination about what is owed and to whom, and begin to make those payments regularly until the balance is paid in full. If the account is past due, be sure to contact the creditor about your intentions to make things right. The creditor may be able to work something out to accommodate your current financial situation.

Of utmost importance, and this is just good financial sense, keep good records to prove yourself right when the time comes. In a dispute, you will be obligated to do so, and the reports will be changed based on how well you present this information.

Numerous agencies offer credit reports. Nine dollars will get you a full report. (*Note:* If you have ever been refused credit, the report is free.)

Innocent missteps can create lower scores. When you do check your report, and FICO will let you do this for a fee, you should close any accounts that you will never use. Closing an open account doesn't make it disappear from your credit report, however.

The best advice available suggests that it is best to keep your credit-card ownership to a minimum, keep balances low (at least below 25 percent of the credit limit), and do your best to fix any credit issues before you begin to search for funds to borrow or insurance.

This can be a major obstacle for some folks. Kim spent almost a year getting her finances in line, consolidating or eliminating (closing) credit cards, paying off short-term loans, and adjusting her spending habits. The dream of a home doesn't have to die with the first setback. For some folks, fixing their credit history can mean a long-term delay in purchasing their first home. By repairing any credit damage, however, you will save money not only on the home loan but also on the cost of servicing those outstanding debts.

Some Things to Remember

- *Any loan is not the best loan.* Too often the lender will come back to you and suggest that there might be a way. They will seem sincere and begin to offer up deals that seem too good to be true. Back away. Quite a few states have passed laws against this type of lending. It is commonly called *predatory.* It is an embarrassment to the mortgage industry, but it still happens. The conduct of these groups is usually restricted to the unscrupulous, but the net effect can cost all of us. Suffice to say, mortgages can be twisted and turned in a number of mind-boggling ways. Always choose the deal that seems the most comfortable. In the lending business, if it seems too good to be true, it definitely is.
- *Get the best deal, not the only deal.* The only way to do this is to get your credit in line. A good risk is always a sought-after customer. Lenders' least favorite job is chasing down delinquent loans. Good credit will have them knocking your door down to make you offers.

ONE FOOT IN FRONT OF THE OTHER

Without a doubt, buying a home will be one of the most intrusive events in your life—and well it should be. There is a great deal of gravity associated with borrowing these amounts of money. Despite the attractiveness of homeownership, the responsibilities that come with it are enormous.

No matter who you are, your financial life will be laid bare in front of you. Nothing is "overlooked," and everything is considered. Lenders are funny that way. Their interest is your financial house, and you are the tour guide. Kim found the process unnerving.

She was prepared to attend the classes required by the city of Vancouver, Washington's first-time buyers program that offered affordable housing and low interest rates. The program offered monetary incentives for staying in the house for 10 years as part of an urban renovation project repopulating the downtown area.

Then Kim had found the house she wanted. She told me that at that moment she was prepared to do whatever it took to get into the house. She wanted it that bad!

She had never been in a home that was hers. She grew up in rental houses and apartments. Once she was old enough to move away from her parents, she rented apartments and houses herself for the next 13 years. She began to worry that she was falling into the same cycle. That growing concern added to the realization that her friends, she told me recently, had all married, bought houses, and had kids. Quite suddenly, all she seems to want for her daughter was her own room, her own yard, and her own house.

I might be stating something obvious, but you should understand that there is a relationship between houses and money. You think that you are buying a house, but in fact what you are buying is a loan. The loan will enable you to purchase the house. In turn, the house you are buying is used as collateral giving the bank something of value to take back from you should you fail to live up to your end of the deal. After getting your financial life in order, it is time to start looking at the financing.

Obtaining financing for your house is a big deal. This is a relationship of the highest financial order. You and your budget are about to meet the folks with the money. When the ink is finally dry, everyone is a winner. The lender will have a new source of interest income, and you will have a roof over your head that 30 years from now you can call your own. The only obstacle ahead of you is trying to be the one who emerges with the best deal.

Kim had been paying $850 a month to live in a rural house almost 30 miles from work. The property was nice, with wide pastures, separately leased to someone else, on every side planted with summer wheat. These kinds of "perfectly peaceful" places can lull you into complacency, and before you know it, years have drifted past.

She asked me at one point to work up some numbers for her. I had no idea what her financial or credit situation was, so I showed her a worse-case (high interest rate) scenario. If she were to secure a 30-year mortgage of $110,000 at 7.25 percent, her monthly payment would be roughly $750, I told her. She seemed stunned. Of course, this figure did not include taxes and insurance, furniture, paint, or any of the numerous other things houses always seem to need.

Kim needed to start looking around at houses in that price range. In my neck of the woods, housing prices have outpaced much of the nation in selling prices. Thus $110,000, unfortunately, doesn't buy what it used to in the past. So it was up to Kim to find a home in that price range and ask herself some pointed questions:

- Is this what my money will buy?
- Is this where I see myself?
- Is this what I had in mind?

Most people bring some pretty expensive dreams and unrealistic notions to the hunt for the right house. This is unfortunate. You end up "settling" for something less. Kim had no idea what $110,000 could buy.

There is a downside to renting. The shared walls and ceilings, communal halls that fill with the odors of other folks' cooking, and the lack of permanency are all good reasons for looking for a house to call your own.

On the other hand, $750 a month in rent might get you some good housing in the right part of town, close to work, and be easy on the transportation budget. Perhaps this allows you to dress better, socialize at a higher level, and attend concerts and shows, all the while paying down college bills and saving for a vacation.

Mortgages change all that. Not completely, but pleasantly. On the next page you will find a table that illustrates the most often given reason for moving from a renter to a homeowner—taxes. As the cost of living and other expenses cause landlords to raise rents, mortgage payments stay the same for the life of the loan.

Savings increase every year because mortgage payments are fixed. This illustration doesn't tell the whole story very well. The first table seems to make renting in the short term a good decision compared with homeownership. But suppose, just for giggles, that we throw in the tax savings. I mentioned this advantage earlier. Look at what kind of money you would save in payments to Uncle Sam over the same period in the second table on the next page.

Rent vs. Mortgage

Years	Rent	Mortgage Difference	Monthly Difference	Yearly
1	800	1000	−200	−2400
2	840	1000	−160	−1920
3	882	1000	−118	−1416
4	926	1000	−74	−888
5	972	1000	−28	−336
6	1021	1000	+21	+252
7	1072	1000	+72	+86

Rent vs. Mortgage – Yearly Tax Savings

Years	Mortgage Rent	Monthly Difference	Tax Savings	Yearly Difference	Savings	Tax
1	800	1000	−200	−50	−2400	−600
2	840	1000	−160	−10	−1920	−120
3	882	1000	−118	+32	−1416	+384
4	926	1000	−74	+76	−888	+912
5	972	1000	−28–336	+122	−336	+1464
6	1021	1000	+21	+171	+252	+2052
7	1072	1000	+72	+222	+864	+2664

Impressive, huh? However, there is more you need to consider and consider carefully. Let's weigh some of the pros and cons.

The Advantages: Buying

Equity

Owning property builds equity. *Equity* is the difference between the remainder of the balance of the loan you might have and the worth of the property. Without getting ahead of myself, the refinancing boom of the last several low-interest years was brought on by rising home values.

These folks found that the difference between what they owed on their homes and the market value had changed, sometimes dramatically in their favor. In other words, their homes were worth far more than they paid for them. Many of these people took their loans back to the lender and asked for better terms and, in many cases, more money. This money is referred to as equity.

Community

Homeownership can provide you with a sense of belonging that no other purchase can. This security comes with a certain stability that isn't offered with renting. As I mentioned before, you will be able to change your property to your liking, improving this community feeling further.

The Advantages: Renting

Mobility

Homeownership effectively removes your ability to up and leave at a moment's notice. If your job opportunities are more fluid, renting allows you to pursue those chances and the changes that come with them much more easily.

Maintenance

When the basement leaks, homeowners must fix it. When the plumbing clogs, homeowners are on their own. When your neighbors become loud or unruly, homeowners have little recourse. Renters can call the landlord or simply move away from the problem. When you own, you are your own lord of the land, and all responsibility falls to you.

The Disadvantages: Buying

Ownership

While ownership "has its privileges," it comes at a price. If the roof needs to be repaired, the cost is borne solely by you. This can be an incredible drain on the equity you think you may have in your home. Your obligation, both to your lender and to your community to keep the property sales worthy, is extremely important. You may think that you will be in the house for a few years, but fortunes change. Keeping your home in good repair keeps the value of your home close to or above what your loan balance is. This is a very important and costly side effect of ownership.

Taxes

Taxes will always be an ongoing challenge. They tend to always go up when it comes to your property. Higher values equal higher taxes. In some neighborhoods, this comes as a surprise. Because of historic low valuations of the homes, taxes can increase substantially if the neighborhood changes. It is very difficult to factor these changes in. It becomes an ever-changing cost of homeownership that few folks understand.

Loss of Equity

Or worse, foreclosure. Many folks have purchased homes that may be beyond their means or may be too costly should their employment picture change. Foreclosure is a painful procedure whereby the lending institution determines through late or unmade payments that you are no longer a good risk for ownership. What they do at this point is take back the property. Not only is this devastating for your credit record, but it also doesn't do much for your personal esteem either. Loss of equity comes when valuations of a neighborhood change due to economic downturns or the inability of homes to sell because no one wants them. Being strapped with a mortgage that may have been increased to pay other debts can lead to serious financial difficulties.

Mobility

Let's face it; you have none. If you want to move, the process of selling is far more complicated than the notice you might give a landlord. I'll go into that later, but for now, you need to understand that buying is not the same as being "foot loose and fancy free."

The Disadvantages: Renting

Taxes

There are tax benefits that come with homeownership. The following are items you can deduct from your taxable income as itemized deductions on both your federal and state income tax returns: annual mortgage loan interest charges, property taxes, and the cost of your loan, called *points*.

Equity

Each dime that goes into the landlord's pocket allows you to have shelter. Nothing more. Although equity is an ever-shifting, sometimes-abstract number, the equity in your home is fully realized after the term of the mortgage expires and you are handed the deed to the home you have been living in all those years. Renting never has this reward.

Costs

Rents can change over time, and very rarely do they decrease. Landlords seek to keep the spread between owning and renting as close as possible. This keeps the renter indecisive about making the move from renting to buying. In 2002, this *spread,* as the real estate people like to call it, was difficult to maintain because interest-rate reductions made purchasing seem like the common-sense move. Weighing the cost differences, many folks who would still be renting might have continued to do so had rents declined in tandem with falling mortgage rates.

Control

Your presence in a building is not guaranteed. If you become a renter that is deemed out of sync with the other tenants, you could be asked to leave. Miss enough rent payments, and you could be asked to leave.

THE MORTGAGE JUNGLE

Before we get going on this journey, it is important to understand that businesses get really picky when large sums of money are at stake. Believe me, you will pick up on this new tension right away.

There are basically three types of lenders. The first type of lender is a *mortgage banker.* Mortgage bankers are not really bankers at all. They offer no other types of loans or banking services, such as checking or savings accounts. What they do is simple: They have a line of credit, which allows them to lend money. Once the transaction is finalized, your loan is sold. Let me explain how this works. By selling your loan, the mortgage banker gets the money it needs to sell more loans. So this is not a bad thing. The terms that you have agreed on are still in force and will last for the life of the loan. Thus the next institution down the line benefits from the sale. The profits in this kind of transaction are made from fees and anything the banker can gain from the sale of the loan. Again, this does not have any effect on you as borrower. The advantage in using a mortgage banker is that a banker may be able to help you get a mortgage in a tough loan situation and may be better able to time a tricky market. The disadvantage is purely paperwork. Should your loan be sold, as a mortgage banker will do, you need to keep track of where your payment is going. My wife is extremely adept at keeping track of these financial doings and is loved doubly by me for doing so. You should follow up on any kind of change. Make sure that checks are arriving at your new lenders in a timely fashion. Remember that those credit-reporting agencies are watching.

Mortgage brokers, on the other hand, have no money to lend. They act as a conduit between you and a lender. These are the companies that advertise heavily in the media. You know the ones. These people can find you four offers in just minutes. The advantage here is that if your situation is relatively straightforward (good credit, high down payment, etc.), using this lender's supermarket is really not such a bad idea. By having offers to choose from, many different lenders present a kind of cool scenario. The disadvantage comes with flexibility. You need to remember that you are dealing with a middleman who has laid out different offers for you. If you need some personalized service on your loan, you will find it in limited supply.

Banks, savings and loans (S&Ls), and the big *national mortgage companies* also sell mortgages, but they have different reasons for doing so. Some keep the loans. Some sell them. Banks and S&Ls act as the collection point for the fees and the payments in these types of transactions. They also make sure that property taxes have been paid.

So much for the lenders. Now let's take a look at the loans they might offer you.

There are basically two types of loans: fixed-rate mortgages and adjustable-rate mortgages.

Fixed-rate mortgages, as the name implies, have the same payment for the length of the loan. This is a nice feature, but it can work as both an advantage and a disadvantage. Your house payment can be conveniently budgeted and planned for month after month. This is good. These come in different lengths of time, usually 30, 15, and sometimes 20 years, with your rate of interest and your total payment fixed over that period. This is also good. However, it can play havoc with your biological clock. Thirty years is a long time. You add your age with your mortgage and have a clear point on the horizon, a day when the mortgage is paid off. When refinancing with a fixed-rate mortgage, be sure to keep that point on the horizon in clear focus. You wouldn't want to add another 30 years until the big payoff, right?

   Adjustable-rate mortgages (ARMs) lock in only a time frame, usually a short one (3, 5, or 7 years), with the interest rate on your loan being adjusted periodically to accommodate the changes in the current market interest rates. Your payment is usually lower, but that can change with time. If you are planning on just a short stay in your new home and want the lowest possible monthly payment, then this might be the type of loan for you. At the time of this writing, the average stay in a home is just a little over 8 years.

   The temptation to take the lower-rate mortgage is often seized on by first-time buyers. The upside here is somewhat of an illusion. You get more house for what seems like less money. The downside to even the most attractive ARM is simple: You will need to look for new financing at the end of the adjustable period. This can be a costly lesson, with fees upon fees piling up, especially if you find that your short-term plans have changed and you want to stay in the house.

Understanding Points

Points are the cost of obtaining a loan at a certain interest rate. A point is simply a percentage of the cost of the mortgage. If you want to understand points, look at it this way: If there are points, usually worth a certain dollar amount per point, paying these upfront gets you the lower interest rate. That rate is used most often in advertising. Suppose, however, that you don't have the money for the points. The tradeoff for points is the interest rate. If you are unable to "buy down your points," you will pay a slightly higher interest rate. Basically, therefore, you are borrowing the points tucked inside your mortgage. If you plan on staying in the house, paying the points will be more profitable in the long run. If you plan on a short stay; paying the points offers no real savings. The average person doesn't really understand this. To the uninitiated, points are the bait and switch of mortgages.

   There are certain fees that you can dodge. You need to remember that you are the customer, and you should act like one. Question every cost.

Lenders have overhead costs that they would like to pass on to you in the form of processing fees, underwriting, wire transfers, and funding. These aren't necessarily your problem.

There are certain fees, however, that you can't dodge. Application fees fall into this category. These usually take the form of appraisal fees and credit-report fees. These fees generally don't exceed $400 and should be, by law, applied as part of the application fee before the lender has secured financing for you.

Good news is on the horizon. There is legislation being discussed that would make disclosure of these fees more readily available to consumers. It depends on how the change is written, but if it is done right, all parties will benefit. You will know more about the costs of the loan/mortgage, and the relationship between you and the lender will be less confusing and stressful.

If things are square with your credit and employment, then you can shop among all types of lenders for the best deal that suits you. However, if your situation is a little sketchy or unstable in your application, a bank or a broker may be better able to help you.

THE MONEY QUESTION

Can You Afford a House?

This is something that you should ask yourself and your financial partner. The mortgage payment for this home is going to eat up about 30 percent of your gross monthly income. Are you comfortable with that idea?

Is a house that you purchase using a simple formula of 2.5 times your gross annual income going to be the house you want? Will it be everything you want, filling all your needs, present and future? At this stage in your financial life, will a small house that you can call your own be enough house for you and, more important, your plans?

Kim wishes that she had really looked at the neighborhood before moving in. Far from being run down, the neighborhood is in transition, and because it would be considered urban, it is in need of development. The terms of her agreement with the city require her to stay in the house for 10 years.

My wife and I bought our present home 20 years ago in a market that was severely depressed. Money was extremely expensive in those days. In other words, those historically low interest rates being advertised at present were not available. Our first mortgage had a 13 percent interest rate. The house, on the other hand, cost us one-sixth of its current value.

I'll have to give her credit; my wife was much smarter about the potential of this house than I was. With any luck, you will have the same good fortune as we did. Even if you don't, though, buying a home is not for everyone.

For us, the problem with the house was unknown until we moved in, and it turned out not to be the house at all. It was *me*. I have a low "Bob Vila quotient." I can't really fix anything. If we had asked ourselves this question prior to buying an old house, we would have been able to calculate the costs that eventually would crop up, many of which were quite large.

Have You Thought About All the Other Costs?

Utilities, maintenance, emergencies, and emergency repairs can start to cripple a financially strapped budget. These costs don't include your plan on personalizing the place. Although it may take years to get the house just the way you want it, you are still going to want to do some things to make it more livable.

Will Buying This House Make You Cash-Poor?

The temptation to buy more than you can reasonably afford might force you to use borrowed money to stay afloat. If it's your first home, you can bet it won't be your last. So don't ruin yourself financially on the first time out. Buy what you can afford.

How Much Money Do I Need to Get into a House?

The biggest hurdle to homeownership is coming up with the cash for the down payment. Lenders traditionally consider this as the commitment by you that promises repayment of the loan. Often this down payment must be 20 percent of the value of your home.

Total closing costs + down payment = cash required

What If You Don't Have a Down Payment?

There is also the chance that you can get that home with no money down. The catch—and there always is one—comes with the interest rate itself.

No money down means a somewhat higher rate than conventional adver-tised mortgages.

There are other places for finding a down payment. One source is your retirement funds. You are allowed a one-time, tax-free withdrawal from your 401(k), 403(b), or IRA to make a first-time home purchase. While this is not the best method, it is certainly an allowable one.

Many first-time buyers seek out government assistance programs such as the Federal Housing Authority, the Department of Veterans Affairs, or as Kim did when she purchased her home, the local department of housing and urban development. Below you will find some of the requirements of these agencies.

Federal Housing Administration (FHA) requirements:

- In most instances, the FHA requires a 3 percent down payment.
- Ability to finance closing costs, but the FHA has set limits on the amounts lenders can charge for some closing cost fees (e.g., orig-ination fee no more than 1 percent of mortgage).
- Maximum mortgage amount can vary significantly by area, a fig-ure that is adjusted on a periodic basis using economic variables.

Veterans Affairs (VA) loan information:

- No down payment requirements.
- More favorable interest rates. This is primarily due to the govern-ment backing provided by the VA.
- Ability to finance funding fee.
- No mortgage insurance premiums.
- Maximum loan amount may be 100 percent of the appraised value of the home, determined by a VA-approved appraiser, or up to four times the VA eligibility entitlement (currently $50,750 with a maximum loan amount of $200,300).

So what are these government agencies? In 1938, the government cre-ated a company known as the Federal National Mortgage Association (FNMA). This government program, called Fannie Mae for short, was to help low-, moderate-, and middle-income families realize what has been referred to as the "American dream"—homeownership. (*www.fanniemae.com*)

In 1968, the company went public (meaning that shares were offered to people who wanted to invest in it), which would allow the company to reach a broader section of the population. The company buys mortgages from lenders and provides money to continue allowing lenders to make homeownership possible for many people who wouldn't necessarily be able to qualify for a loan. Congress continues to provide the charter under which the company operates but provides no financial backing. This government connection allows the company to operate under the guise of being federally backed, giving borrowers and lenders alike added security in the process.

The Government National Mortgage Association (GNMA) or Ginnie Mae (*www.ginniemae.gov*), provides a link between capital markets (the lenders) and the federal housing markets. Ninety-five percent of all home loans through the FHA and the VA are backed by GNMA. What this means to lenders is the promise that they will get paid, even if the borrower doesn't make the payments and defaults on the loan. This government backing allows lenders to make available loans in rural and urban areas that are not considered the most desirable by lenders. Ginnie Mae is the lending branch of Housing and Urban Development, which is the enforcement arm of the federal government that ensures that housing and the purchase of housing is a nondiscriminatory event.

HUD is involved with the government as the strong arm of the Fair Housing Act, helping communities develop and grow into livable and viable places. The branch of HUD that works with lenders is the FHA. The FHA provides the loans, which have limits, but the down payment requirements are usually lower than for conventional loans. The goal behind HUD is affordability. The government wants homeownership to become a reality.

And then there is Freddie Mac (*www.freddiemac.com*). This is also a governmental creation, and in fact, the president appoints 5 of the 18 members on its board. Like Fannie Mae, Freddie Mac provides money to lenders to continue their efforts at selling mortgages.

How much house can you afford? It all has to do with interest rates. If rates go down a quarter of a point (0.25 percent), you can buy about 2 percent more house. If they go up, you buy 2 percent less house. It is important to note that I am using 7.25 percent in these samples, which was until recently a much more historic rate. As I pen this, rates for a 30-year mortgage are at 5.67 percent. They certainly can go lower depending on a variety of reasons, but much lower is not considered the norm. Thus, using the same 30-year fixed-rate model and a $1000 per month mortgage payment at 7.25 percent will get you a $147,000 home.

$1250 per month @ 7.25 percent buys a home worth $183,000.
$1500 per month @7.25 percent buys a home worth $220,000.
$2000 per month @7.25 percent buys a home worth $293,000.

Therefore, with your preapproved mortgage in hand, or at least some idea of how much you can afford, the hunt begins. For first-time buyers, I suggest that you use an agent. The best way to find one is to ask family and friends if they know one, have had a good experience with one, and would recommend one.

When Is the Best Time to Refinance?

For most of us, our home is the single biggest investment we will make. Like many homeowners, you will scrimp and save and then spend and spend, just trying to maintain it. When the value of your home increases, this is called *equity*. This "paper" value can represent money, real cash that was available for just about any purpose. When interest rates are low, people begin to use this equity to pay off credit-card debts, take vacations, or even to free up money to invest. While this has become acceptable practice, it is not a good use of equity. Refinancing involves a new loan at a larger amount with a lower interest rate. Using a 30-year loan to pay for a vacation, pay down debt, or worse does not make any real sense, even if it has become common practice. Refinancing to lower your mortgage payment is a good thing. Using the difference to pay down credit-card debt, save for a vacation, or squirrel some additional money into your retirement plan is a good outcomes of a wise refinance. Using the money to reinvest in your home, increasing the value of the property, is another good reason to consider refinancing. If your interest rate drops a full percentage point, this may be a good time to consider refinancing.

Carefully evaluate your motives for borrowing against your home, the length of time it would take to repay the debt, and the possibility that you might have to walk away from your home with a lot less in equity. Use refinancing the way it was meant to be used: to lower your interest rate so that your overall mortgage payment will be less. Don't use it to increase your debt.

The costs and time are the biggest factors. I have discussed the why and the why-nots, so taking the next step is not all that difficult. The process is very similar to the one you took when you purchased your home. You first must have your debt in line, and then you must qualify for the mortgage.

Is Your Home an Investment?

Yes and no. To understand why this answer is "yes and no," it helps to understand liquidity. *Liquidity* is, in the simplest of explanations, the ability to sell an investment whenever the time is right. Stocks are liquid. Homes are not.

There are other differences between real estate and the stock market when they are compared side by side as investments. For one thing, real estate isn't always valued properly. Down markets, where your house can be worth much less, can occur without warning and can last longer in certain parts of the country than others. While you are losing value in your home, you continue to put money into it. The old adage that a "house is only a hole in the ground where you throw money" will never sound as true until you own one.

A stock is liquid because it can remain invested until you decide to sell. It is this ability to take your profits or cut your losses when you see fit that makes stocks attractive as an investment. While both are priced based on supply and demand, houses are much harder to sell.

Don't get me wrong; homeownership can't be beat for long-term peace of mind. However, when you compare the two in terms of investments, homeownership just isn't the same.

DRAWING CONCLUSIONS

Buying a home requires a good deal of understanding about who you are, how well you handle money, and most important, how you handle your obligations.

- This is an enormous financial undertaking. People get swept up in the ability to buy a house; the money available to them is intoxicating. Having a home is a status symbol. But the costs of a house can be staggering and may turn into a slowly building financial problem. If a money problem is going to take your relationship down, it probably will be the house that caused it. Carefully examine your plans and your expectations. While losing a house is not the end of the world, sacrificing a relationship in the process is.

- Kim told me the other day that she is putting in a new heating system. In the 3 years that she has owned her home, I have been entertained by her stories of home repair, the building of her deck, and the landscaping. Sure, she struggles. She scrimps and saves and has had to make adjustments, but she has never regretted buying her home.

- Whenever a bump in the financial road befalls a member of the blue class, the effects can be devastating. We spoke a good deal about credit in this chapter, and it has become increasingly important to monitor how your credit is reported.

- In 2003, over 10 million people suffered from some type of credit fraud or identity theft. Although the average bill for such a crime is about $5000, you will have no trouble finding individuals with stories of identity theft that nearly destroyed them financially. Add in the psychological effects of having to prove that you are innocent to these creditors, and you can see that this is no easy ordeal to experience.

- This crime is getting more common every year as more strangers have access to your vital information. Using a shredder to destroy your documents is a start, but you have little chance of catching some low-level data-entry clerk from selling your vital statistics.

- The best defense: Check your credit report once a year. It is a small investment for peace of mind.

5

Step 5: Learn Disaster Self-Defense

J orge once told me that the real game in insurance is trying to guess what is enough without paying one single penny more for coverage you won't need. To Jorge, it is all about protection. An affable and talkative man, Jorge has delivered the mail to our home for 10 years. He has the usual assortment of policies that come with adulthood, and then some.

In this chapter we will take a look at the paradox that is insurance. We need it, but we are loath to think about it. We can't afford it, but at the same time we probably can't afford to live without it. There are far too many people out there who are without the necessary insurance they need to live a less worrisome existence.

Answer this:

Insurance is . . .

a. A scare tactic whose products seem to cater to every possible type of fear we have, sold by agents who seem to care using a veneer of concern when in fact, the product you buy is money in their pocket.

b. A gamble by both you and the insurance company. (The gamble is simple. You will need to be able to determine the right amount of coverage for any possible injury, pain and suffering, loss of life for you and your family for the duration of the policy for the foreseeable future and the insurance company that because of who you are, what you do, or even how you play needs to determine if you are worth the risk all the while hoping you will never need it.)

c. All of the above.

d. None of the above.

Unfortunately, the answer is c. If you look too close, the commissions made on these policies and the profits generated by them make insurance seem nothing but a scam. On the other hand, insurance is about protecting the things that become near and dear to us. It is the realization that the baby in the crib needs you, that the car you purchase needs protection from other drivers and thieves, and that the "living wage" that you provide will be missed by your family if you are injured or die. It means protecting the very things that you hold close to you—the things that you have collected around you.

We are going to take an overview of what insurance is, when and if you need it, and how much of it you need. This is a tough assignment. We'll start from the first brush you may have had with the subject—your car.

AUTOMOBILE INSURANCE

The following e-mail, "Haven't Slept since 2 A.M.," was waiting for me the other day from my 27-year-old son:

> We were heading to El Caporal for dinner last night at 7 p.m. when we pulled up to the stop sign at the intersection of Aubrey and Portland Ave. We had to wait a minute for the cars to pass in order to swing a left onto Portland. All is clear and I started to make the left turn when literally out of no where a huge pickup truck appeared parallel to us on the driver's side going about 40 with tires screeching attempting to stop.
>
> The truck avoided smashing into the driver's side door (my door with Martin in his car seat behind me) by about 6 inches. There are three large trees on the SE corner of that intersection in which this truck smashed head on and bounced about 6 feet off of. We sat in the middle of the intersection for about 2.5 of the longest seconds. I realized that we were just gawking when the bits of broken headlights and tree bark started bouncing off the cement.
>
> Seconds before, I had looked in my rear view mirror while we were waiting at the stop sign and there was absolutely no one behind us. At night, you can see if a car is coming down Aubrey because of their head-lights. I have no idea where this truck came from.
>
> It seemed like something from the movies where the secret service cars come out of nowhere and are really close to the car forcing you to

pull over. I heard the tires skid before I even saw it. I slammed the brakes and our car stopped immediately without really a jerking or anything since I had just started to pull out.

This truck had been going so fast that within a few seconds it had made up the difference from the bottom of Aubrey Butte to the intersection. We still don't know if he was trying to go around us to continue straight and by me turning it forced him to slam his brakes and turn his wheel slightly.

Semicautiously I approached the truck, where the driver was getting out and coming around to the passenger side to help out his girlfriend/wife (we don't know). I asked him if he was ok, and he calmly looked at me and said yeah. That's it. His friend was hurt in the truck but talking. He opened her door, and she got out limping and in obvious pain.

By now others had come by from their homes, and one lady who was jogging up Aubrey St. had come all the way back when she heard the crash. She says that they were going about 50 in a 25 M.P.H. zone. The guy is standing there just stunned looking at his truck, while the girl just walked off down the street.

He goes to get her, and the next thing any of us know is that they are hauling ass down the street. Police came and that was that. No clue what the deal was with the two in the truck.

I had the enchiladas and a perfect margarita.

André

This unusually lengthy note, different from his to-the-point variety allowed me to relive many of the close calls that have happened to me on the road. All but two I was able to avoid, the ones involving contact did much worse to my car than to the other driver's car. And fortunately, no one was injured.

Jorge learned the cost of insurance early on also. When he was 17, he borrowed his mother's car, a new 1970 Chevy SS. The car was far faster and newer than the old Ford he owned. On this casual drive, he received his first speeding ticket. That ticket did more than cost him a month's worth of gas money. It raised his insurance rates and keep them high until he was 25. Understanding the way car insurance works shouldn't be the result of using their services in filing a claim or, worse, finding out that their rates have increased because of a ticket or driving infraction.

Purchasing car insurance is often our first brush with the industry, usually as a teen. This initial contact reveals much of how the insurance industry operates. Insurance companies gather statistics by the boatload, and from this information, they then deduce not only your "risky-ness" but also the probability of trouble ahead. Always looking at the glass as half empty, this industry deals with tragedy and how to predict it.

The insurance industry spends enormous amounts of money collecting statistics. Companies use these numbers to gauge the likelihood that a driver will react a certain way. For the insurance business, it is how a company determines the wager. If you are in a group that has statistically driven poorly, then that information suggests that you are probably a greater risk.

I once made my kids a similar wager. The odds were pretty much tilted in my favor, though. The offer was simple: I would pay for their insurance if in return they gave me a 4.0 grade point average (GPA), or straight A's. It is important to note that they all turned out to be upstanding, law-abiding, tax-paying citizens (as far as I know, anyway), but none of them took the offer. I figured, much like an insurance company would do, that if you are an upstanding student with a high degree of scholastic drive, then you also would be a good driver who understood consequences, actions, and reactions and would be better prepared for what might happen in a somewhat more forward-thinking manner. The theory remains untested to this day.

The cost of the least expensive policy is based on the highest standard of driver. This would be someone like the perfect student, similar to the one in my example above. The cost increases as the standard is reduced.

Insurance companies do nothing more than make educated guesses based on historic results. If you smoke, that information suggests that you probably will live a shorter life, possibly with illnesses, than someone who refrains. Not everyone who smokes necessarily lives a shorter life, but statistically, such a person is in an abbreviated life group. If you are a teen, there is a far better chance that you don't understand the risks of the road or have the experience behind the wheel to make quick decisions. Adults, whose time on the road will have built a better base of probable situations, are considered a better risk than their younger counterparts.

Automobile insurance policies break down as follows.

Obligations, Coverage/Liability, Rights, Limitations

Obligations come under the heading of *deductibles.* The deductible is the amount of money that you will pay out of pocket before the insurance kicks in. The more you have promised to pay on your own in the way of something called a *deductible,* the lower is your overall premium. Your premium is your monthly, quarterly, or annual insurance payment. Increasing the deductible is one of the ways to make your insurance coverage more afford-able. Deductibles usually come in increments ranging from $100 to $1000 and are paid by you first, with the remainder of the costs paid by the insurance company. Thus, the more you pay, the less the company has to pay out of pocket, and this means a lower monthly premium for the insurance. It also works in reverse. The lower the deductible; the higher is the premium.

How you determine your deductible rests purely on your ability to pay in the case of an accident. A lower deductible, while attractive to those with little in the way of cash, will result in a prohibitively higher premium.

Coverage or liability involves the tricky part of insuring drivers. *Liability* is the damage you cause to others and their property. *Coverage* can include medical payments, damage to your own car, and even protection from an uninsured or underinsured motorist who may happen to be involved in the accident. The cost of your policy will depend on what type of coverage you opt for or are qualified to get. A good agent will factor in statistics about you, your car, your driving habits, and where you live. There is also the age factor, which adjusts your premium downward after age 25, assuming that you have a good driving record.

Currently, five states do not require minimum liability coverage. The states of New Hampshire, South Carolina, Tennessee, Virginia, and Wisconsin, while not mandating that you carry liability coverage, strongly suggest that you carry some. States that do require a minimum amount will not allow a driver in that state to purchase less. It is always a good idea to buy more than the minimums. Let me tell you why.

The basis for automobile liability insurance is to protect you from litigation should you do damage to someone else's car, property, or person. I have no way of knowing how much time you spend on the road, but even with as little driving as I do, the roadways of this country seem to be cluttered not only with distracted drivers but also with automobile operators who do not seem to realize how much of a weapon their cars really are. Each accident is unique. Each driver must be aware of the enormous amount of information that needs to be processed quickly and reacted to accordingly in driving.

Liability can't prevent you from having an accident, but it can protect what you own. Inadequate liability coverage puts the things you have accumulated in your life at risk, especially if you have a serious accident and your liability coverage is inadequate. Courts will look at your assets, such as your home, your savings, and anything else they can garner, to pay for the mishap.

Insuring a car for its replacement value, while attractive, is not very wise. Cars, as many of you know, depreciate the minute they are driven off the lot. Older cars have no real blue book value. *Kelly Blue Book* values are the automobile "bible" for dealers trying to make determinations of the value of a car based on its make, model, and age. Admittedly, the love you feel for that older-model car of yours is unfounded monetarily, according to the "blue book" numbers. It may just sadden you to realize how worthless everyone else considers "your baby."

Leased cars have higher insurance costs due to the returned-vehicle value. If you lease a car, any damage done to it will need to be corrected to make it as good as factory new. This means that factory-certified parts, a more expensive option for repair, will be used in repair of the vehicle.

Cars that are purchased with financing also will require repair in the case of an accident, but only for aesthetics. You will get a check whether you repair the car or not. What you do with it is your own business. It will be up to you and your agent to figure the right amount for this reimbursement.

It does not end there, though. Medical payments can be added into the cost of your coverage, covering you and your passengers when you drive your car, operate another person's car with his or her permission, or find yourself in an automobile accident as a pedestrian.

So far we have covered some of the basic ways you can keep your insurance premiums at a reasonable level. Here's a summary:

1. Carry higher deductibles. (This means having at least that amount available for out-of-pocket expenses.)
2. Drop collision and comprehensive coverage on cars that are worth little, and shop around for the lowest prices.
3. Buy low-profile cars that have air bags and other safety features, including antilock braking systems.

4. Group other insurable items with the same company (e.g., insuring more than one car and possibly using the same insurance company for life and homeowners coverage).

5. Drive defensively (no traffic infractions).

These considerations all can help to get those premiums down to a manageable level. To a lesser extent, where you live will have some effect on your rates but could increase your costs in other categories. For instance, living in a rural area may be cheaper but will add mileage and drive time if you work in the city.

And then there is the car you buy. This can greatly affect the cost of the insurance you purchase. The following tables list the most and least expensive cars to insure (based on 2002 models), and surprisingly, they aren't all "expensive" cars.

Ten Most Expensive Cars to Insure

1.   Mitsubishi Montero Sport
2.   Chevrolet Corvette Convertible
3.   Lexus GS 430
4.   Cadillac Escalade
5.   BMW 7 Series
6.   Honda Civic Coupe
7.   Chevrolet Corvette Coupe
8.   Mitsubishi Mirage Coupe
9.   Toyota 4Runner
10. BMW 5 Series

Ten Least Expensive Cars to Insure

1.   Buick LeSabre
2.   Oldsmobile Silhouette
3.   Honda Odyssey
4.   Buick Park Avenue
5.   Pontiac Montana
6.   Mercury Grand Marquis
7.   Buick Century
8.   Chevrolet Venture
9.   GMC Safari
10. Oldsmobile Bravada

The most expensive list has cars that are most probable targets of thieves, more inclined to produce bad crashes and rollovers, and are leaning more toward luxury than not. The least expensive list has cars that tend to be safer, less attractive to thieves, and less inclined to cause extensive damage to other cars involved in accidents. In addition, they will be less likely to draw lawsuits for additional damages in the same way an expensive luxury car might, a car that is a symbol of its owner's wealth.

One final note about automobile insurance has to do with your credit scores. Chapter 4 discussed the Fair, Isaac and Company (FICO) scores that can be used to determine your interest rate should you apply for a loan. Over 350 U.S. and Canadian insurers have contacted this company to enable them to better provide premium pricing to their customers.

This has drawn the outrage of many consumer groups, as well as state insurance commissioners, who find the practice appalling. They suggest that a driver's financial well-being is no indication of the quality of the driver. Financial hardship from a lost job, medical problems, or divorce has no effect on how a person reacts in traffic situations.

Jorge and I talked about this very subject the other day. He thinks that the financial well-being of a driver is not necessarily what an insurance company is looking at when it examines the FICO scores on your credit report. He calls buying insurance a simple financial transaction. When you purchase insurance, you strike a bargain with the insurer: If it agrees to pay a claim, you should be good for the deductible and be counted on to make the premium payments.

Jorge is right, and you should take notice of the way credit boo-boos can turn up in the least expected places. Wherever money is transacted, your creditworthiness is never assumed.

The upside is all good. If you have some control over your financial well-being, this new means of determining the cost of insuring drivers based on credit scores can work to your advantage.

RENTERS' INSURANCE

It doesn't matter how or why you rent. You may be a first-time renter because you are moving away from home for the first time, because you are being forced to relocate to obtain work, or because your marriage has

Insurance: At What Age, When?

Indicator	Age
Car insurance	16 years until . . .
Renters' insurance	
Health insurance, without kids	
Health insurance, with kids	
Disability insurance	
Life insurance	

failed. It doesn't really matter. You are probably sharing a building with many different people. You have common walls, common floors, and common ceilings. You have the semidisabled man upstairs that you never met who sometimes falls asleep in his chair. Did I mention that he smokes? There is the elderly lady living below you who keeps her water for tea hot on an old portable burner. There are a couple of guys living next door. These are your neighbors. These are different people from different walks of life that are oblivious to your existence, much as you are to theirs. But, as they say in the insurance business, mishaps happen.

Just for a minute take a look around your apartment. As you survey your domain that may or may not be furnished with second-hand chairs, Goodwill tables and lamps, and shelving made from cinderblocks and old boards, you may not see much worth keeping. And then you look closer. You see your entertainment system. You probably have a computer with peripherals, a portable sound system, a cell phone, a camera, digital or otherwise, and other valuables that you probably don't think of as much more than "stuff." The replacement value of this "stuff," the cost of getting you back to this exact point, sentimentality aside, is not small. Your "stuff" is worth something.

Jorge tells this story to every renter he knows. He is the biggest seller of rental insurance policies I know, and he isn't even an agent. His stories usually are embellished, with those neighbors becoming reckless or worse, robbing you while you are at work.

Probably one of the most overlooked and inexpensive ways to introduce yourself to being insured as an adult is with renters' insurance. Talk to the agent who handles your car insurance first. You probably know him from conversation before and after you bought your automobile policy. Get other quotes, by all means, but often the agent you already do business with can give you something of a break called a *multiline discount.*

Jorge never fails to complete his tale, one that does involve quite a few scary stories of his days as a renter, without giving his audience some basics. Without a doubt, the first thing that you should do if you find yourself renting is to do an inventory. Look around your place. Figure out what you own, and write it down, film it, or do something to record ownership. Then take your rental agreement, your car title, your tax returns, any loan documents, and that newly created inventory with pictures or movies of all of your stuff and high-tail it over to the bank and rent a safe deposit box.

This sounds simple, but it is overlooked by far too many people. You will rent that box or one like it for the rest of your life. Jorge will tell you that his box has papers and agreements, recent tax returns, baseball cards, and a videotape that is boringly narrated as he walks from room to room, focusing in on item by item, categorizing each and every piece. During any insurance inquiry, he is convinced that the insurance company will settle just to make the tape stop.

There are two basic policies in this business. *Actual-cash-value policies* take into consideration the value of your property in a claim and base the payout on what it is worth now. In other words, the insurance company assumes that whatever you own, no matter how valuable you think it is, is actually valued at a far lower amount. *Replacement-cash-value policies,* on the other hand, are more expensive from a premium standpoint, but they give you your life back based on the cost of replacing your property—provided, of course, that you can prove it. This is why you need to keep all the proof to support your claim in a safe deposit box.

Your renters' or condo insurance policy will come with a number. For renters, it is HO-4, with condominium owners getting HO-6 policies. There is nothing special in this information, just some of the lingo you will confront in the process. Next will be the events from which you need to be protected. It's amazing how many of these things can happen to you once you consider it.

The Top 15 Insurable Events

- Fire or lightning
- Smoke
- Vehicles
- Theft
- Explosion
- Windstorm or hail
- Vandalism or malicious mischief
- Water-related damage from home utilities
- Damage by glass or safety glazing material from a building
- Aircraft
- Falling objects
- Weight of ice, snow, or sleet
- Riot or civil commotion
- Electrical surge damage
- Volcanic eruption

Floods and earthquakes didn't make the list for good reason. In all the catastrophic occurrences that could happen, insurance companies have determined that the events on the list are possible, but not probable, and certainly insurable. In other words, there is a good chance that an earthquake or a flood can be more catastrophic and should cost more. This kind of additional coverage is called a *rider*. Riders are common for both renters and homeowners, allowing you to upgrade your coverage without rewriting the entire policy. If you live in an area that is prone to either floods or earthquakes, or other events such as hurricanes, then the additional coverage might be worth considering.

Your basic policy usually will cover inconvenience payments to you to live somewhere else until whatever happened to your apartment or condo is repaired. According to the Insurance Information Institute, the cost of the average renter's coverage will be between $150 and $300 per year. This covers your personal stuff and you against liability up to $300,000. Extremely valuable items will require a rider or a different policy. If something happens in your apartment, you can be sued. Liability coverage protects you from these kinds of ugly problems. Where you live also will dictate the cost of your policy. Ownership of some breeds of dogs could be costly as well.

Having insurance does protect you from the problems I mentioned earlier and will mention below, but it comes at a cost.

Jorge, in his never-ending quest to get the best coverage for the least amount of money, has uncovered what he calls a "very objectionable practice" by insurers. The insurance industry has begun a practice of opening a claim with only an inquiry of coverage. This means that when you call an agent to tell her that your camera was stolen from your apartment, a claim is opened. If you later find your camera or choose not to pursue the claim because your deductible covers the replacement, the insurance company counts this as an open claim. If you have too many of these claims, you might find yourself with a canceled policy or higher premiums. And this kind of dubious activity will bring out the bad side of Jorge, an otherwise affable gentleman.

The only available solution so far is your judgment. If the claim is small or your deductible will pay for most of it, you probably would be wise to avoid opening the claim. The insurance industry has adopted this policy without much fanfare. Assess the value of your damage, your deductible, and the worth of opening a claim based on what I just told you. Save your policy for the big claims, the ones that are the most financially damaging.

Insurance: At What Age, When?

Indicator	Age
Car insurance	16 years until . . .
Renters' insurance	18 years until . . . homeownership
Health insurance, without kids	
Health insurance, with kids	
Disability insurance	
Life insurance	

HEALTH INSURANCE
Norman Rockwell Was an Insurance Salesman

He wasn't really. His classic prints of life, the cherished moments he captured, could have been used to sell insurance. They pull at our heart with a strange strength, reminding us of what we see our lives as, what our lives could be, or what we want to keep them being. Who of us hasn't seen Rockwell's famous *Freedom from Want,* the elderly grandparents serving a huge, perfectly cooked turkey to an anxious and happy family. Insurance is about protecting yourself and your loved ones.

Something psychological separates us from all other living organisms. We worry. We can, all by ourselves, run best-case and worse-case scenarios in our heads. Insurance removes the financial downside for worry. It can't prevent the fateful events that await you from happening. It can only reimburse you for your monetary loss.

Recently, Jorge asked me if I were in a situation where I overheard a conversation on whose topic I could add some good information, would I interrupt? No, I told him, I would write about it. He nodded and told me about his experience at work one day.

He had walked into his small office and found two women comparing notes on health insurance bills. Overhearing their conversation was one of those unavoidable moments, he said, and it made him uncomfortable to eavesdrop. Both women had opted for a policy that would allow them to choose their own doctors. The cost to them was what was left after the insurance company paid the first 80 percent. They had a yearly deductible that had to be satisfied before the insurance company began to pay. What became obvious after several minutes was that neither of them totally understood the other's policy options, and neither completely understood her own policy completely. Insurance can be a minefield of bad choices—not necessarily bad policies, but poorly matched customers. In the complicated category of health insurance, folks like these two women are commonplace. This fact alone drives Jorge crazy. Maybe he should have interrupted them. He is slight man with a polite manner and an infectious smile—and an obvious passion for insurance. He might have saved them.

Everyday, folks are forced to choose between one policy or another, different coverages, and varying degrees of costs and preferences. These decisions do not come without consequences.

We all need health insurance of some kind. The questions are what kind and how much coverage do we need. I am going to walk you through a step-by-step explanation of what this costly insurance is about, whether you should live looking over your shoulder, or whether you should sleep at night without so much as a care. I am going to give you an overview of your state's health policies and, even more important, try to give you enough information to get your kids insured, stay insured once you have a plan, and know what to do if you decide to retire before waiting until Medicaid kicks in to help.

So where does this leave us? If you are between the ages of 18 and 24, you probably have determined that insurance is not worth the money. You are, after all, young, healthy, and full of the ability to embrace life to the fullest. And you are probably right. However, the growing ranks of uninsured, of which this group boasts the largest number, could end up costing the rest of us more.

Dr. Jeanne Lambrew, an associate professor of health policy at George Washington University, and Dr. Arthur Garson, Jr., of the University of Virginia, conducted policy-relevant research on Medicaid, Medicare, the uninsured, and long-term care and have offered suggestions that can help the growing number of uninsured in this country. In 2001, they reported that the number of uninsured Americans climbed by 1.4 million people. (Chart below indicates percentage increases.)

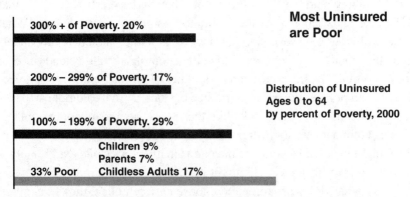

Most Uninsured are Poor

300% + of Poverty. 20%

200% – 299% of Poverty. 17%

Distribution of Uninsured
Ages 0 to 64
by percent of Poverty, 2000

100% – 199% of Poverty. 29%

Children 9%
Parents 7%
33% Poor   Childless Adults 17%

Source: Commonwealth Fund task force on the Future of Health Insurance, analysis of March 2001 Current Population Survey

By dodging the cost of insurance, you are probably going to run the risk of being unable to seek medical help when you need it. Doctors Lambrew and Garson report that the largest group of uninsured Americans falls into the 18- to 24-year age group. They also point out that the number of folks who are aged 55 to 65 years (when Medicaid kicks in) is quickly closing in statistically. This also counts workers who are in between jobs and have lost their coverage. Changes in their employers' benefits have added many folks to the growing list of the underinsured.

The underlying reason for lack of coverage is mostly poverty. With 43 million Americans lacking coverage in 2003, the number of Americans who lack coverage at different times throughout the year masks the real problem facing the industry. Young folks face what the industry refers to as "family transition problems." They may have left a home that covered their health needs or simply aged their way out of a program. This lack of ability to pay doesn't lessen the risks for this age range.

This young group of uninsureds, almost twice as large as that of uninsured children and 28 percent of the total uninsured population, is faced with low-paying entry-level jobs that don't offer insurance. This group finds itself making 40 percent less than full-time, full-year workers. Faced with such information, there are some basics you need to know before you try to bridge the gap between having nothing and becoming insured. Let's first break down the basics of what health insurance coverage is all about.

   Individual policies. These are policies for yourself or your family that are separate from a plan provided by an employer, a union, or some other professional group with which you might be associated. You may have one if you are self-employed.

   Group policies. These spread the costs and risks over many people in the same plan, in effect lowering the costs of the plan for each member.

The following describes each basic plan, and each has some cluster of letters attached. It isn't particularly important for you to know what each of these abbreviations means, but it may be important if you are beginning to search for an individual policy. Moreover, if you have a group policy, knowing what some of these letters stand for will help you to identify some of the basics of your plan.

Traditional Indemnity (FFS)

This plan is a costly alternative to full coverage and is the preferred coverage for those who either have money or think they are in relatively good health. There are, as you would expect from any plan whose coverage is based on flexibility, higher premium payments, scads of additional paperwork, and more money out of pocket. The flexible part of the plan comes with your ability to choose your own doctor. This type of plan allows you to see a specialist without first being referred by a primary care physician. The two women Jorge described earlier have this type of plan.

The deductible tends to be prohibitively high, with the insurance company's obligation to pay starting after you have spent upwards of $1500 or more of your own money first. Then the insurance company kicks in a percentage of your costs, usually 80 percent, with the remainder of the tab falling to you. In other words, if an office visit costs $200, you would need to come up with $40 from your own pocket. Some companies require you to pay the full cost first, and they reimburse you after the fact. This requires you to submit the bill to get the 80 percent returned to you.

This will be the first time I mention "reasonable and customary expenses." These expenses, determined by the cost of the same service provided by other doctors in your area, may be the basis for which your reimbursement will come. An expensive doctor will mean that more of the out-of-pocket expenses will fall your way.

Health Maintenance Organization (HMO)

Take away some of the flexibility, such as picking your own doctor, and you have an HMO. Many HMOs will require you to pick a permanent doctor, sometimes known as a *primary care physician* (PCP). Other characteristics of this type of plan are the smaller copayments (your out-of-pocket expense), a minimal amount of paper work, and a good amount of preventative health care, some with improvement programs.

There are drawbacks to HMO programs, and you will hear many from those who have converted from a plan that allowed them more freedom.

HMOs tend to keep you within their circle, disallowing payments to doctors outside their network and requiring a referral from a PCP before you see a specialist.

Point-of-Service Plans (POS)

POS plans are similar to HMOs with some exceptions. Each difference will cost you additional money out of pocket. For instance, a POS plan will pay for an outside doctor, but the amount of coverage is greatly diminished from the coverage provided for doctors within the network. A network, in case you didn't know, is usually doctors and clinicians that the organization prefers you visit. A POS plan will require that you first get permission from a PCP before you go outside the group. Without this permission, you can end up paying all or most of the cost of the visit.

One of the upside offerings of a POS plan is the preventative programs designed to keep you healthy. These programs, in turn, keep overall plan costs lower.

Preferred-Provider Organization (PPO)

A PPO plan wants you to stay within its network by offering financial incentives to stay, such as lower copayments for routine visits during regular hours, permission-free visits to see a specialist within the group, and the ability, in most instances, to pay the difference in costs between a doctor outside the PPO and one in the PPO.

Consolidated Omnibus Reconciliation Act (COBRA)

You will hear this term used in reference to interim insurance coverage. If you have lost your job, this short-term safety net legislated by Congress in 1985 allows you to continue to participate in the group plan provided by your employer for up to 18 months. Conditions that apply may be a cut in hours or the actual end of your employment—provided, of course, that you parted ways under reasonable circumstances. In other words, if you are without a job due to gross misconduct, you are also out of insurance for yourself and your family. It should go without saying that this safety net has helped many families in need on a short-term basis. (It also should go without saying that you should behave yourself on the job. This is one of those unknown penalties for stupidity.)

COBRA also allows spouses and children to continue coverage for up to 36 months in a variety of circumstances, such as death of the employee, divorce or legal separation, or the employee becomes eligible for Medicare. This last instance has become of great concern lately as the age group of dependent spouses or early retirees finds themselves uninsured from 55 to 65 years of age. As the boomers hit these years, the number of folks who will fall into the ranks of the uninsured in this country will soar. But that's another story.

This less than prefect plan is not mandated for employers of fewer than 20 employees. And the premiums you will be required to pay will be about 2 percent more than the full premium. If you have questions about COBRA, contact your regional or district office of the Pension and Welfare Benefits Administration of the U.S. Department of Labor. These people usually can give you greater information about your individual case. In some states you will find that extended benefits have been enacted, charmingly referred to as *mini-COBRAs.*

Without a doubt, the health insurance issue will provide an elected official the accolades of many if he or she can figure out the perfect plan. This plan would be inexpensive. It would allow superior care with the doctor of our choice.

Pregnancy further complicates the issue. Not all plans cover maternity, and if they do, they may neglect to include prenatal or well-baby coverage. This is an especially important consideration if you are changing jobs and need to continue coverage uninterrupted. Senators Nancy L. Kassebaum (R-KS) and Edward M. Kennedy (D-MA), working with HMOs, introduced an important piece of legislation designed to allow workers to change jobs without fear of losing insurance in the interim. This act, often referred to as the Health Insurance Portability and Accountability Act of 1996 or *HIPAA,* is especially beneficial to those who have some sort of preexisting condition that was not covered at the preceding job, those who have been discriminated against because of genetic information, and those who have been declined coverage for any other reason. HIPAA requires a new employer to continue maternity coverage for you if you change jobs but does not require your employer to do so if you have no current clause for pregnancy. Nor does it require your employer to match the coverage you once had.

However, you are not without options. You could still be eligible for a COBRA plan from your previous employer while the waiting period for you new coverage expires. There is just such a policy, called a *guaranteed issue policy,* and it is designed to cover folks who previously had 18 months of continuous group coverage. These laws basically guarantee coverage, but the insurance industry, clever as it is, has created a special high-risk pool of people for whom it feels entitled to charge higher premiums. Often the waiting period (usually 6 months) and restrictions for entrance into the pool run by industry officials can be prohibitive for a pregnant woman.

There are ways around this 6-month waiting period, and they are addressed on a state-by-state basis. For those who qualify due to income limitations, Medicaid can cover a good deal.

Now that you can talk the talk, as the saying goes, where does this leave you in terms of actually deciding where to commit the cash you will need to get the coverage you desire? You are probably a little scared at the consequences of not having coverage and probably a little pragmatic about the costs. Some folks think that saving the premium they may have paid will cover any problems they might face down the road. Can anyone else see the flaws in that thinking?

Let's discuss some of your options.

Get with a group plan. Better yet, get with a good group plan. The sheer numbers of people in the plan drives down the cost of the plan for individuals. Even in the face of soaring health costs (for whatever reason), members of a group insurance plan still pay considerably less than people with individual plans.

If unions are good for one thing, it is their ability to bargain good health coverage for their participants. Companies who fight these organizations do a great disservice to the state of health care coverage in the United States. As long as Wall Street applauds companies that deny their employees the chance at healthier lives in the face of profits, this gap between insured and uninsured workers will continue unabated. The rising costs, however, are causing problems at the bargaining tables where unions argue for their members. This should not be a labor relations issue. It needs to be solved in Washington.

Outside such a group, an individual policy is the only option available to those who earn a certain level of income. As an individual, you are not guaranteed insurance. Preexisting conditions can prevent you from getting insurance at all without joining high-risk pools. Some health conditions will increase your cost, and this can be just as prohibitive.

Jorge will be the first to tell you that there are as many ways to write an insurance policy as there are stars in the night sky. Quotes can vary widely for the same coverage from different insurers. It costs nothing to shop around. Be prepared to become discouraged. If you can take advantage of COBRA coverage, use it while you begin or continue your search.

If you currently have no coverage, probably the most important thing to consider is your asset base. Assets are otherwise known as possessions. You shouldn't believe that if you have nothing in the way of assets that the cost of being uninsured will not fall on you. Doctors and hospitals are extremely diligent when seeking repayment for services. If you are of low income, you may qualify for federal or state programs. Even if you don't make use of the service, sign up.

If you make more than the minimums for assisted coverage, a policy with high premiums or one with partial coverage is better than none. As I mentioned in the section on renting, once you look around at what you own, the cost of replacing it can surprise you.

There are things that you need to ask yourself first. Be honest. Afterward, you can deduct those "must haves" when you find out the cost.

Your current physician, if you have one, might be part of a network, such as an HMO or a PPO. If so, this is good news. You may want to look into that organization. However, another group may cost less. This may force you to choose another physician and ultimately decide whether the cost of that sort of a preference is worth it.

If you require visits to specialists such as a chiropractor, for example, each plan has limits to its coverage. This may be a determining factor in your purchase.

How much is too much? The coverage you want can be determined by the blanket of security you want to wear. If you are young, without kids, and have managed to put away a few dollars along the way, you probably could get by with a basic policy. The reasoning goes like this: The times you find yourself in a physician's office are so infrequent that the out-of-pocket expense (paying the deductible) may be manageable.

Insurance: At What Age, When?

Indicator	Age
Car insurance	16 years until . . .
Renters' insurance	18 years until . . . homeownership
Health insurance, without kids	20 years, basic coverage
Health insurance, with kids	20 years, affordable coverage
Disability insurance	
Life insurance	

DISABILITY INSURANCE

Destiny Is Not Bad Management

Charlie Brown once said, "I've developed a new philosophy. . . . I only dread one day at a time." In a perfect world, we all make it to retirement. We live a long life without mishap and without running out of money. We are able to leave to our children a wealth of memories and maybe a little of our financial legacy as well. Wouldn't this just be too perfect?

In a perfect world, there would be no need for any insurance products because, well, everything would be risk-free. But our world is not perfect. Reluctantly, we give into the need for insurance.

Unfortunately, we all need insurance of some kind because insurance is more than peace of mind. It is the realization that there is something else to protect in this world than our own hide. However, when we think of insurance, we think of life.

I had purchased my first life insurance policy at the age of 32. I found myself completely immersed in the subject. Quite a bit of that research became one of the catalysts for the creation of my first Web site, *BlueCollarDollar.com*. And this was how I first met Jorge. Financial writers tend to get money questions the same way doctors get medical queries, I suppose. Jorge and I happened to be at the same St. Patrick's Day party. What, he asked, did I think of disability insurance. I had to admit to him that I hadn't really thought much about it. Until then.

What I had overlooked was the little-talked-about insurance that covers injury. Sure, I was well aware that workers' compensation insurance would take care of me should I be injured on the job. Thus 23 percent of my week was covered. If something happened to me while I was driving, I was taken care of through my automobile insurance. That's another 2 percent. What about the remaining 500 hours of my typical working month? How, if I was faced with injury that did not allow me to return to work and was not covered by workers' compensation insurance, would I be able to cover the costs of living that have accumulated over the years?

Jorge's insistence and my own curiosity pushed me to begin to investigate disability insurance. This is the insurance that covers a serious, disabling injury off the job—in other words, when I am on my own time. The odds of a person having at least one long-term disability that lasts 3 months or longer before that person reaches age 65 are as follows:

Age	Probability
25	44%
30	42%
35	41%
40	39%
45	36%
50	33%
55	27%

In addition, according to the 1985 Society of Actuaries, the following table shows how many people have recovered, died, or remained disabled for 5 years after a disability onset.

Age at Onset of Disability	Recovered	Died	Still Disabled
25	44.1%	9.7%	46.2%
35	34.0%	12.3%	53.7%
45	21.5%	19.9%	58.6%
55	11.8%	28.5%	59.7%

As I began to look for a product, I was introduced to all sorts of troubling statistics. For instance, did you know that 12 percent of all adults are laid out by some sort of disabling injury during their working careers? An incredible number of those folks are injured seriously enough to keep them from returning to the job for 5 years or more. At my age, the probability that I will be injured runs almost 40 percent, with a better one in two chance that the injury will finish my career.

It is important to remember here that I am looking for insurance that will cover me for the time I am away from the job. I could be hanging holiday lights or cleaning the gutters or simply trip and fall down the cellar steps. My inability to perform my job because of an injury is what disability covers. It is coverage for the time when I am not on the clock.

I found out that through my union I have a disability policy that would provide my family with $600 per month (before taxes) for 6 months in the event that something like this happened to me. This would mean that I would get 75 percent less income, and after 6 months, if I haven't recovered, the money would stop. Suppose that I wasn't able to return to work? This is how insurance works on your psyche, haunting you with what-ifs and supposes.

You do need to ask yourself some questions first. How much reserve cash can you get together in the event of a prolonged injury? The commonly recommended 3-month reserve might be fine for some folks but not for anyone I know. For me, keeping 3 months of emergency money available was not possible then and is barely possible now, so reserve money could not be counted on.

I know that every financial guy or gal you meet will recommend having 2 to 3 months' salary set aside for these kinds of emergencies. If you do, that is wonderful. Your self-discipline is to be admired and envied by the rest of us who, even though we save, manage debt, clothe and feed our families, take vacations, work hard, plan for the future, and occasionally enjoy a beer on a late summer afternoon, will never have 3 months' salary in one place.

Back to the topic at hand. I called the insurer who carried the group policy for my union and asked if I could purchase additional coverage. No, they responded. The coverage, I was told, was awarded for the group, and at that time, the company was not extending coverage on anyone's policy. The group policy the union carries is referred to as *guaranteed issue*. This means that policyholders are not required to take a physical examination as a condition of coverage. Before I could ask, the voice on the other end of the phone added that the company was not selling individual policies as a supplement.

No, I thought, was not an acceptable answer to someone who was interested in the company's product.

Perhaps you may be unaware, if you work and pay taxes on your earned income, that you have a disability policy. In fact, Social Security is primarily a disability policy with retirement protection. Thus I called my local Social Security office and actually talked to someone about the coverage provided. The man on the phone said (and I am paraphrasing), "To collect from this office, you have to be so disabled that collecting for death is easier." This is more than likely where they coined the term *living death*. He went on to explain that you have to prove that you can't work. Eighty percent of those who apply get turned down for benefits.

Therefore, I found a list of highly rated insurers and started my search. I had criteria for the policy I was looking to purchase. This insurance would have to be inexpensive. It would have to provide an income that would sustain my family. It would have to cover me for a minimum of 5 years, and if I still couldn't return to the job, I wanted to be retrained at some other occupation. I wanted a cost-of-living adjustment built into the policy. I wanted a benefit that covered at least 50 percent of my income. The people who write these policies will not provide total income protection.

I was laughed off the phone by the first ten companies on my list. The odd part about purchasing disability insurance is its association with your profession. Even though you are asking to be insured for the time you spend away from the job, it is your occupation that determines your premium. The more dangerous your profession, I was told, the higher is the risk, and the higher is the premium. This was the roadblock I was facing.

With the eleventh company I struck gold. I found an agent, a gentleman named Charles Black, who would at least provide me with a quote. However, it wasn't even close to the figure I had in mind in the way of a monthly premium.

Disability insurance breaks down into several parts. Monthly benefits usually are fixed, and extra coverage costs more. Policies are written in two ways. There is the *own occ* phrase, which, in the disability business, means that you are unable to perform the duties of your own occupation. *Any occ* refers to the ability of the insured to gain employment in any job within his or her educational range, thereby qualifying the insured for benefits.

These policies all come with waiting periods, which is a predetermined time before your benefits begin. This allows you to negotiate some of the premium costs based on this time period. Typically, these policies last from 6 months to 2 years. The longer the waiting period for payment after the claim is filed, the cheaper the insurance premium will be. Some of the better group policies can kick in immediately or take as long as 2 weeks. Delays in payment are usually a result of the need for some proof that what is wrong is truly disabling. Individual policies, like the one I sought, would not start payment for 6 months, just about the time my group policy would stop paying. With any luck, the disability wouldn't last that long. This is also the point when finances start to take the deepest cuts. Of course, this is where your ability to survive for a short period of time without an income comes in.

Leading Cause for Short Disability Claims

- Pregnancy (normal): 20%
- Pregnancy (complications): 9%
- Injuries (excluding back): 9%
- Back injuries: 8%
- Digestive/intestinal: 8%

Source: UnumProvident.

The next time I spoke with Mr. Black, I was more specific on how I wanted the policy written. "Suppose," I said, "that the policy kicks in after the 6 months. Suppose that the policy covers only my occupation [which is meat cutter]. Suppose," I continued as he listened intently, "that we have a rider attached to the policy stating that if I qualify for Social Security, your company would be off the hook for 80 percent of the monthly payment." I told him that I wanted the policy to last for 5 years at 50 percent of my income, with cost-of-living adjustments built in at 2 percent for the first 5 years. I wanted it to be noncancelable, and I wanted what every disability insurer wants—to get me back on the job even if I needed to be retrained.

Now sometimes you actually can get the insurer to write such additions, called *riders,* into a basic policy. I knew, though, that working in one of the highest-risk groups, I was pushing the envelope asking for what I wanted.

Much to my surprise, Mr. Black's company went for it. The policy is noncancelable until I am 65. I will receive full payment after 6 months unless Social Security kicks in. I get my benefit increase of 2 percent for the first 5 years. The cost of the policy to me is $1.03 per day.

For the average worker, one in a less hazardous occupation, the cost of disability insurance can be inexpensive. Like all insurance, the premiums will be based on FICO scores, your health and occupation, and what amount of coverage you want. Start looking with your employer. Your company may be able to offer you an extended policy through your group. If not, look to your own insurance company. It may be able to give you a reasonable multiline quote. If you think you can do better, use that quote as the basis for shopping around.

Insurance: At What Age, When?

Indicator	Age
Car insurance	16 years until . . .
Renters' insurance	18 years until . . . homeownership
Health insurance, without kids	20 years, basic coverage
Health insurance, with kids	20 years, affordable coverage
Disability insurance	If you own a home or condo or have a family
Life insurance	

LIFE INSURANCE

Actually, It's Actuarial

An actuary is a person who, if you're drowning in a pond 20 feet offshore, will throw you an 11-foot rope and point out that he's meeting you *more than* half way.

Or

What's the difference between an insurance company actuary and a mafia actuary? An insurance company actuary can tell you how many people will die this year; a mafia actuary can name them.

Or better yet

An actuary, an underwriter, and an insurance salesperson are riding in a car. The salesperson has his foot on the gas, the underwriter has her foot on the brake, and the actuary is looking out the back window telling them where to go.

I met Dede before she became an insurance agent, when she was a housewife with three active boys, one of whom was good friends with my youngest son. It's funny when you think back about some people, the things you remember about them. She was married to an Oregon lobbyist, whom she later divorced. They owned a house whose front door actually was on the side of the house. The back yard was an in-ground pool. The only land left after the pool was installed was the slim concrete walkway around the perimeter. Her oldest boy could, I was told, jump into the pool from his bedroom window.

Our boys met at a Bible study class held on Sunday afternoons. This class was made up of the children of parents who were either lacking in the ability to pass down religion to their youngsters or simply wanted them to learn the untainted version. The only other thing about Dede that I remember is that I knew more about life insurance than she did.

She happened to be working for the company I wanted to do business with, and because I like to make sure commissions go to people I know, I chose her. The company, not that it matters in the general course of conversation, was New York Life. New York Life is what is referred to as a *mutual company,* meaning that the policyholders wholly own it. Many insurers have demutualized in the last several years. In essence, this means that as a policyholder, you also become a shareholder.

When I picked that particular company, and this is by no means an endorsement, I was picking from a group of five large and trusted companies that looked to be financially solid and dependable. You want a company that will be there when you die in who knows how many years.

Picking your company and your policy will require a little homework on your part. I will tell you throughout this book and if I ever meet any of you that any financial transaction entered into by a blue-class worker is more important than one entered into by a much wealthier person. You don't have the money to make too many financial mistakes. You are entitled to make some, but too many mistakes can be ruinous.

Buying life insurance is one of those tricky moments. Not only is the company you choose important but also what you know about your policy. What your life insurance policy becomes is a transfer of wealth, a built-in protection designed to help your survivors after you have passed. In the next few pages I will walk you through some of the basics of life insurance.

Theotis talks about himself in the first person and speaks with a deep, gravely, Dizzy Gillespie voice. He is a large man who is quick to laugh and has seen more than anyone's fair share of hardships. He lost his father when he turned 18, and as the oldest of 11 children, he was left with his mother and the responsibility of looking after all of them. When I first met Theotis, he was planning on another Christmas with this family. All 11 grown kids and their families were to gather this year at his house with his own family of five. "Fifty-six people," he said, "and we will eat more than just one ham, let me tell you. Specially after spending all morning worshipin' the Lord!"

He told me once that he had learned two things about life: He knew that he would always have folks depending on him, and he would never be rich. Theotis told me about a boss he once had. This man, he said, took the young Theotis aside and told him that as long as he had so many people depending on him, he should have insurance. "Buy it young," Theotis said, retelling the story, "before you happen to get old or worse, come down with somethin' uninsurable." He spoke about this as he stood at the smoking grill that is the lifeblood of his underground restaurant, an unlicensed backyard feast for the senses. I heard about his barbecue sauce from Jorge, of all people, and was finally permitted to go to his house to try it. This illegal operation was by invitation only, which means that if your name is on the list, all you need to do is call and ask if you can come over. Twenty bucks gets you all the ribs you can eat, an ear of corn, and cold fresh lemonade.

"Ol' Jim told me to buy whole life and never let up payin' on it." Theotis had six slabs of ribs on the grill that literally were sizzling flavor into the early evening air. Theotis' ribs even sounded good.

"I didn't ask him why, but he said too many people dependin' on you son, and chances are you will never be able to save too much 'til it's too late." He turned the slabs on the grill through a haze of spice-rich smoke.

He added that he has changed the beneficiaries on his policy eight times. "Once I had all my brothers and sisters listed." He laughed deeply, saying, "Woulda been fun watchin' them fight over it from up there." As he slathered the meat with his own recipe sauce, he did agree that the man had been right. "All I have is that policy and this house. Every dime I have supports the two oldest boys in school, and the three younger ones are just gonna haveta stand in line."

Life insurance paints a perfect world with some of the pieces missing. "Ol' Jim" goes by many names, and a lot of us have met him. He's someone we respect or admire who offers us some piece of advice. What he told Theotis was just good common sense. His father left him with nothing but hungry mouths aged all the way down to a 4-year-old brother. This blind trust in that man's advice has let Theotis sleep a little more comfortably all these years. Because he purchased his policy when he was still a young man of 20, the premiums are insanely inexpensive. Thirty years later, he still pays the same premium and tells me that he's got a "heap of cash value built up."

Life insurance companies provide us with a variety of choices. Some work out really well. Some are of questionable nature, preying on the vulnerable and inexperienced. I want to take a minute to lay out some of the basics of these policies, ending with the most complicated of inventions by insurers, the annuity.

First, life insurers like you to be healthy when you purchase your policy. A healthy person means less risk. Less risk means less likelihood of a payout. It doesn't eliminate the possibility; it just reduces it. The insurance company will require a medical examination. Your rates may depend on the outcome of that examination. If you smoke or engage in any other life-threatening activity, your policy will be seriously affected in terms of overall cost. An implied suggestion here is that if an insurance company considers what you do to be risky, it probably is.

Second, insurance protects those you love from the loss of your financial contribution. If you are young and unmarried, you do not need life insurance despite the attractiveness of the low cost. If you have started a family or otherwise have someone that is dependent on your financial well-being for their financial comfort, you will need coverage.

That said, let's look at the different types of policies available.

Often the first type of insurance you encounter will be a *nonguaranteed term life*. This kind of policy, which is designed to provide nothing but a death benefit, is used for a special limited purpose. It is commonly used to cover some outstanding monetary commitment such as a mortgage. Policies can be structured in a variety of ways. Mortgage protection can offer decreasing coverage over the length of the outstanding balance at a fixed premium. This means that as your mortgage decreases over time, so does the coverage. Nonguaranteed term life insurance also can have premium increases. If your health should take a turn for the worse during the policy period, renewal can be extremely difficult and costly.

Annual renewable insurance is called *convertible term*. These policies are more attractive for those who want a longer fixed time period but require the expense of the policy to be low. They actually qualify as two separate types of policies despite many of the same characteristics.

The annual renewable type can have fixed premiums for 10, 20, or 30 years. Convertible policies can be "converted" to permanent policies. If the cost of the premiums for another policy at this later point in your life looks as if it might be excessive, or if your health declines during the policy-holding period, converting the policy to a permanent one may be your only option. This is the policy of financial planners.

Convertible policies are inexpensive. The common argument in favor of these types of policies goes something like this: If you buy inexpensive insurance, you will be able to direct more money into other investments that will have a greater historic return. The argument holds sway over those who feel savvy enough to believe that the markets will be kind enough to them or they have the personal discipline to stay on track, invest regularly, and create wealth that will replace the policy when the term expires.

The next category of policies comes with a new set of criteria for the buyer. In the business of permanent life insurance, it is all about the company you chose. This is not to diminish the importance of the insurer of term policies, but your agreement with such insurers tends to be of a shorter term timewise than that of the insurer of permanent policies.

Permanent life insurance policies come in three basic flavors. The *whole life policy* is as much of an investment as insurance should get. The payments are fixed throughout the lifetime of the policy. This spreads the costs over an incredibly long period. During this period, your monthly payment pays a good deal of the cost of the policy up front for the first several years. After that, more and more of your premium dollars are invested. Much to my surprise, this is the kind of policy that Jorge has. He bought such a policy for two reasons he told me after I recovered from the shock. This is the same guy who always wanted more (coverage) for less (money).

He told me the investment side of the policy intrigued him. Whole life policies are exactly that, a policy you keep for life. These types of policies actually build a cash value that can be sizable enough that the policy itself will begin to pay the premiums. All the while, the policy value or death benefit increases. The death benefit is the money your beneficiaries receive when you die. Jorge has had the same policy for 10 years, and his return, the difference between what he pays in premiums, which in a whole life policy is invested, and his cash value has been about 7 percent. This, he says, has given him some early investment discipline and a policy that cannot be canceled. Choosing the right company is almost more important than the least expensive one. If you plan on being with a company for 50 years or more, you want one that will be around as well.

Universal life policies do some premium investing also, and likewise, it is important to choose the right company. With this type of policy, there is a good deal more flexibility.

The death benefit, which is the money paid to your survivors, is more flexible, allowing the policyholder to adjust it up or down. Often, little more than medical proof that everything is okay will allow you to increase this benefit. Universal policies require that you keep the policy funded. This requires a little discipline on your part to be sure that the payments you make are adequate to keep cash in reserve. This is not a good choice for the absent-minded.

Take the two flavors above and blend them together, and violá, you have a *variable life policy*. This insurance policy, not for the timid or the apprehensive, will require you to pick investments for your premium dollars, and the returns from these investments will determine the cash value and the death benefit.

If you choose to go this route, be sure to get a guaranteed minimum death benefit. In a good year, you can laugh in the face of this guarantee. If you do poorly in your investment choices, this will at least leave something for your beneficiaries. As a word of warning, avoid the temptation to borrow against any of these policies. Often a healthy cash value can look attractive, especially in times of monetary need. Resist. You are not Congress borrowing from Social Security. You have to pay it back, or your beneficiaries, the very ones you bought the policy for, will face a diminished payout.

Sleight of Hand

Annuities are part insurance and part investment. The sum of both parts and the complexities they throw at the average investor are not, in my humble opinion, worth the effort. But what if you have no choice?

Some of you have annuities as part of a 403(b) plan, a plan similar to a 401(k) offered to teachers and public-sector workers. I will get into the nuts and bolts of this type of retirement plan later on, and I probably should save annuities for later also. However, the industry that sells these

---

Insurance: At What Age, When?

Indicator	Age
Car insurance	16 years until . . .
Renters' insurance	18 years until . . . homeownership
Health insurance, without kids	20 years, basic coverage
Health insurance, with kids	20 years, affordable coverage
Disability insurance	If you own a home or condo or have a family
Life insurance	When someone depends on you

products is likely to be your insurance agent, posing as a financial planner. So let's get out the scalpels and start slicing this multilayered product open.

I can't begin to tell you the number of people who have written to me over the years asking for advice on how to get out of their annuity. Much of what seems like an adverse opinion about this product is based on the passion in those letters. Annuities were always sold to these folks as a great investment idea laden with guarantees of fixed returns.

Sold as a retirement planning tool, annuities are a little of both and not enough of either. How this works seems incredibly simple. When you first buy an annuity, you enter into what is referred to as the *accumulation phase*. This is where you pay premiums as you would with a regular insurance policy, and this money earns a rate of return. After years of paying this premium, you retire, and the second step kicks in—the *annuitized phase*. This is where the annuity begins to pay you back your money plus interest until you die.

Now for the fun part (and kudos to the insurance people for being able to sell something like this to the general public). The resemblance of this product to an insurance policy is murky at best. The death benefit is there, but it is based on the value of the policy before you annuitize (start receiving payments). In an attempt to simplify this further, the death benefit is based on your account value or the amount of money you have paid into it, whichever is greater. The mutual fund part plays a significant role here. Good choices followed by good returns all equal a healthy annuitized payout period. When the reverse happens and your investments don't do as well, the burden of the insurance company's guarantees falls back on them.

Based on your choice of investment options, the "performance" of your annuity at your death, before you annuitize, is what your beneficiary would receive. Annuities offer to repay what you have paid in, your principal, if your account value is less than what you have paid into the policy.

When you finally decide at 65 years of age that you want to begin to withdraw a monthly benefit from your annuity, the life insurance part of the equation stops. You no longer will have a death benefit once you begin to receive payments.

Another clever selling point is the tax-deferred status of the account. All the money contributed to the plan grows and isn't taxed until you begin withdrawals. Then the annuity payment is taxed at regular income rates. The theory behind tax-deferred accounts assumes that your income tax rate will be lower after retirement. We'll discuss this later in greater detail, but for now I'll explain simply what this means. By not paying taxes on your investments, by deferring them until later in life, it is widely believed that your income will be less than when you were working. This is not, however, a steadfast rule. Usually, most retirees do earn less, and this lower tax bracket acts as a savings from the higher tax bill you might have paid while you were working.

Annuities penalize early withdrawal, especially in the early phases of the policy. If you should wake up one morning and realize that an annuity may not be the best option for you, the exit costs are quite hefty. These are called *surrender charges*. This prohibitive penalty for exiting the plan generally is applied in the first 7 or 8 years of ownership. Called a *contingent deferred sales charge* (CDSC) or a *back-end sales load,* this fee makes it difficult, not impossible, to get out of the policy once you are in it.

At the time of this writing, there are three basic types of annuities with several offshoots of the variable type. This is not to say that this won't change. Those insurance people are pretty clever and inventive. These products fall into the following groups: fixed, variable, and equity-indexed.

Fixed annuities are a problematic type of investment for the insurers. By tying your hopes to the efforts of the investment markets, you risk a good deal if those markets don't cooperate. Offering incredible fixed rates to attract investors/policyholders, these companies paid dearly when the now historic market known as "the bubble" finally burst. With your policy attached to a fixed rate of return, this "conservative but safe" investment did quite well during those down years, much to the dismay of the insurers. Too bad.

The closest cousin to the fixed annuity is the *equity-indexed annuity*. In this particular little gem, you can add value to your fixed account by using the performance of a particular stock index to earn additional interest. Most companies use the most common names in the index business, such as the Standard & Poor's 500 Index (the 500 largest capitalized companies in the United States), for example.

Thus the opportunity presented by an equity-indexed annuity can be both good (you can earn a few extra dollars if the market is performing well) and bad (if the market does not perform well, you basically have a fixed annuity).

I should point out, though, and we will delve into this in greater detail further along, that there is still a place in this investing market for investing for the long term. Tying your annuity to an equity index should be done with a long time horizon to average out the bad years with the good. Historically, equities can do quite well. (Let's finish with insurance first before we get to equity investing.)

Throw these types together, add more flexibility to the owner of the annuity to direct his or her investments himself or herself, and you have a *variable annuity.* These plans break down into two subaccounts to further confuse the product.

I don't like these plans for several reasons. The basics of these accounts seem simple. You pick the investment based on your risk tolerance. Few people know what this is. *Risk tolerance* is a highly subjective and personal evaluation of what you think you can stomach in terms of investment performance. I'll get to risk tolerance in more detail later, but why should it play a role in your insurance? Thus, as you buy a policy, you may be asked to pick an investment as well. Based on those picks and their performance, you can make gains to your policy/investment. Conversely, you can lose. Be careful of added costs for trading between accounts. The final downside kicker deals with annuitization period. The payment you receive will change with performance of your investment picks, which can range from aggressive to conservative. The insurance company will provide you with recalculations on a yearly basis.

The cash value of the account needs to be maintained in these subaccount annuities. When the policyholder chooses an investment among the many products offered by the industry (over 2500 are currently offered, ranging from index funds to growth to fixed-income funds), the investment must keep the cash value in adequate balance to cover mortality and expenses (M&E) fees. If this falls shy of the needed balance, the insurance company will request that you increase the funding in the account through increased payments. In other words, if your investments do badly, you will be required to ante up enough cash to keep your M&E fees covered. It's like adding insult to injury.

We're here. We are talking about annuities. It's only fair that we talk about the one place you are most likely to find these types of investments: 403(b) plans. Unlike their 401(k) brethren, these plans seem to attract an inordinate number of annuities within their plan options. The other difference between the two is with the employee. 403(b) plans are tax-deferred retirement plans for employees of educational institutions and certain nonprofit organizations. 401(k) plans administer private-sector employees. 457 plans, while we are on the subject, are for local and state government workers, firefighters, police personnel, and public school employees.

If these plans are the only ones available at your place of work, by all means, take advantage of them. With a long time horizon and some prudent investing, these plans can do as well as private-sector investing. These plans tend to have more hidden costs that can directly affect the return on your investments. This usually requires a little more work on your part. Reading the prospectus in these investment plans is important in any investing situation. In annuities, companies will bury many of these costs. If you know what you are looking for, keep searching until you find them. Otherwise, ask someone where the fees are listed.

As we progress further into this book, the subject of fees will come up. Nobody is going to do something for you, i.e., invest your money, without some charge. Fees are a fact of life. And they will require more than just a flippant remark to explain. The goal here is to try to get the biggest bang for your buck for the lowest possible fee. I'm sure that I'm not the first person who has told you this. I just want to be the last.

However, when it comes to annuities, the fees are out of control. The variable annuity, as we have seen, allows you a great deal of flexibility in controlling your money. This is important because those assets, properly directed, are needed to keep the policy in force. Thus the investment you pick will need to be the best possible.

The average charge for subaccounts in a variable annuity, according to Morningstar, is over 2 percent. This is what the insurance company charges you.

By way of example, if you had, say, $1000 in an annuity, you would, after 10 years, have earned $90 less than if you had had the same money in a mutual fund with the same assumed 10 percent return. Of the $1.2 trillion in annuity assets that investors have in these kinds of policies, there is potential of hundreds of millions of dollars lost. These insurance people are a tricky bunch indeed.

The M&E fee covers, among other things, the commission paid to the broker. Then throw in the contract maintenance fee, which is about $30.

Fixed annuities and the policies that are equity indexed do things slightly differently. The fees are subtracted from the assets and reinvested in the annuities. This helps to cover the cost of the guaranteed rate of return they promise you.

I mentioned at the beginning of this section that I received numerous letters about annuities. The letters were largely concerned with the cost of getting out. There was desperation in their notes that made it difficult for me to answer. I told them that you could get out in two ways. Switching to another annuity, or if you want to pay the 10 percent capital gains tax, you could switch it to a life insurance policy, usually without any additional charge. However, there was no way to dodge the first 7 years of the contract and the infamous surrender fee. This little gem of a charge is your payment for parting ways with the insurer, protecting it from an early exit. This little fee starts out charging you 7 percent in the first year should you wish to dissolve the relationship. This is a penalty against your assets. The fee then slips to 6 percent the following year, decreasing a point each successive year.

Some Parting Looks

Homeowner's insurance is part of the home-buying experience. No one will lend you money unless you insure their investment. The best place to get homeowner's insurance is from someone with whom you already have a relationship. If you bought renters' insurance, chances are the agent who helped you will be able to walk you through the process. Otherwise, ask someone like Jorge, your friends, and your family for an agent whom they might recommend.

The two insurances are not wholly different. In an apartment, you insure your things and you insure against anyone getting hurt there (liability). In the rental situation, the landlord insures the property. Become a homeowner, and you now need to cover not only your stuff but your property as well.

The cost of your homeowner's coverage will depend on where you live. If your house is in the path of a hurricane every year, expect to pay for additional coverage. Is your humble abode built where it has flooded in the past? Is the town you decided to live in subject to possible seismic activity? All these naturally occurring problems play into the cost of your policy. Factor in such details as where the closest fire hydrant is, what type of material your home is constructed of, and how many smoke alarms and fire extinguishers you have. These all play a role in your policy's costs. (By the way, you cannot have enough smoke detectors or fire extinguishers.) Well-placed security protection, being a nonsmoker, and keeping your deductible high all can save on the cost of these policies. As with all insurance policies, if you remove much of the risk, the company will remove much of the cost.

An insurance agent will walk you through the complicated process of buying a homeowner's policy. The most difficult part is determining the type of protection. Remember to revisit your policy every couple of years. Take a video of your place, and put it in your safe deposit box.

Your best insurance rates start with you. The way you care for your health can mean a small fortune to you when you enter into the world of insurance. Smokers tend to pay more for the same coverage than non-smokers. It is totally up to you if you smoke, but this is a strong economic argument against the wisdom of it. The costs of insurance are going to continue to rise as long as we use the services of insurance companies more often than we should. Well care is the best medicine.

DRAWING CONCLUSIONS

Most of us cannot flirt with disaster. We are not extremist, nor are we willing to take unnecessary risks. Admittedly, though, we don't want to think about it either. Insurance can offer some peace of mind. It can't stop something terrible from happening, but it can help with the financial end of the problem.

- I asked Jorge to sum up, if he would, his thoughts about insurance. He suggested that it is important to approach insurance the same way you dress. Life without insurance is like being naked. It may feel good, but you are vulnerable. Protecting yourself with life insurance, even the least expensive policy, and making sure that damage to your belongings is covered, are much like a shirt and pants. All the other insurances just add additional protection. Health insurance is like a warm coat according to Jorge, citing the often-used description of life as a "cold, cruel world." Disability insurance and any other additional or better coverage should be based on your ability to pay. Each layer, beginning with the essentials, can make life easier. At least you will be covered from the elements.

- Bringing good credit health to this financial transaction will net you the best deal. If your credit picture improves, ask your company to review your rates. If it doesn't, you might find it necessary to shop for a better deal. Be sure to ask for multiline discounts, a break for bundling all your policies with one company. As Jorge said, treat your insurance purchases as layers of protection. Start with the basic coverage and improve on the quality of the policy as your income or the value of your assets improves (i.e., remodels, expensive toys, etc.). Stick with companies you know. You want to be able to contact your company in the event you need your policy. I understand that every great company started as a small one, but when it comes to insurance, I like experience.

6

Step 6: Plan to Retire on Your Terms

Here we are at a sort of halfway point, perhaps not in pages but at least in a psychological way. We have spent the first half of this book looking at the way we deal with money and the consequences of handling it, the mind-set we need to develop, the debt we need to harness, the budgets we need to shape and form our lives around, the protection we need, and the shelter we require.

So now what? A popular business program on CNBC that airs in the hours before the markets open, "Squawk Box," has heard it all. In an attempt to distance itself from those cheerleading days recently past, the show has taken issue with certain left-over abstract terminology. Such catch phrases caused the host of the show, Mark Haines, to arm himself with a toy "laser" gun and zap anyone who used them. Among the sayings that were repeated far too often by too many guest analysts, mutual fund managers, economists, and station regulars was the term *moving forward*. I suppose that, at my own peril and acknowledging the chance that I may be zapped, commandeering this phrase for the purpose of our discussion is worth the risk.

Essentially, this is what we are going to do—move forward. The firm footing we discussed in preceding chapters allows us to make an easy transition to the next step in your investment life. Before we move forward, though, we need to develop a plan. Once again, we will look at what we know and add to it. If you know very little, this will help you with the understanding you will need in the next chapters. This chapter isn't as long as some others, but it is every bit as important. How you see yourself, as well as what you can expect in your future, can make or break all your efforts at developing financial stability.

YOUR FINANCIAL DIORAMA

Two words drove fear into my very being as my wife and I herded our kids through elementary school—*art project.* I will be the first to admit that I lack the basic gift of being able to bring raw materials to life. I can sketch. I can tinker with music. I think I can write. But when that grade school-aged child comes home with instructions to build a Native American village, I am struck with horror. We find a shoebox, turn in on its side, and look for a starting point for our diorama.

That little Greek word, derived from *dia,* which means "through," and *horama,* meaning "what is seen," seemed to be the project of choice for far too many grade school educators. How can a child, whose world is so small, create a visual picture of an event or a slice of nature without ever having seen anything from a stepped-back perspective? Those teachers can't fool me. This was *my* project—one of those parent-child homework/bonding experiences.

Louis Daguerre created the artform itself in the nineteenth century. And he patented his invention, whose simple design was a revolving platform engineered to give his film, the *daguerreotype,* depth and a three-dimensional "feel." In 1880, the American Museum of Natural History created an environmentally accurate portrait of a bird group using wax for the fauna and bird specimens preserved by taxidermists. This was a glorious display that used the talents of background artists, wildlife experts, and numerous other people who were obsessed with the accuracy of their depictions. They preserved places and animals as they no longer exist. If you should ever find yourself in New York, a visit to this museum is worth the effort.

Creating a similar snapshot in time is important for you in order to understand where you are going financially. Making a diorama of your financial life will require, I am happy to say, no artistic skill.

My friend Mick told me the other day that he never pictured himself as old. That important error in his plan—that lack of vision to think beyond where he happened to be working at the time—has left him working harder than he should. Don't get me wrong; every elderly person in the workplace has not been forced to get a job, but far too many have found themselves in positions similar to Mick's. Instead of chasing golf balls around the links, Mick is chasing shopping carts around a parking lot.

Now is the time to start building that retirement diorama, and to do that, you need to picture yourself retired. This will require you to do three things—be able to see the past, the present, and the future.

There is an old Russian joke that goes something like this: "The future is assured. It's just the past that keeps changing." But that, according to Mick is wrong. He believes something Mark Twain wrote in a letter in 1876: "I said there was but one solitary thing about the past worth remembering and that was the fact that it is past—can't be restored."

So who is right? Up to this point, we have visited a great many things that make your monetary past relevant to your future. What the opening chapters of this book have done is build the initial shape of your financial diorama.

Much like my fumbling fingers working with paper and glue inside a shoe box attempting to help my kids construct art, you are bound to make mistakes. And we have found that many of these mistakes can be corrected. But what does your diorama look like once you have reached the point where the past and the present merge?

Your diorama is a snapshot of where you are right now. This is not easy to pinpoint. The present has a way of captivating us with its rhythms. We get up each morning, head off to work, earn money, come home, prepare meals, and eventually rest, for the next day's coming, and those regular events repeat themselves. This continuity gives us comfort. It also lulls us into complacency.

Over coffee, Mick and I discussed the pitfalls of his lack of planning. I have learned to look forward to his liberal use of "Twain-isms." He told me that he found great solace in Twain's musings and often used his writings "without giving the man the credit due." Mick's biggest regret, he told me, was that he all but missed the warning signs. "You feel good. You think the boss likes what you are doing. And then, suddenly, you're the old guy out." He said that he had fallen victim to the comfort of consistency.

"There are those who would misteach us that to stick in a rut is consistency—and a virtue—and that to climb out of the rut is inconsistency—and a vice," he said, this time giving the credit to Mr. Twain but unable to say where he had read it. "I should have taken a closer look around me when I was younger," he said, sipping from his cup. "I'd a done things a little different."

The future is based on the decisions we make today. We move along through our day-to-day activities, methodically and predictably, without understanding that our horizon is changing.

Mick held the belief that when he retired, Social Security would be an adequate replacement for his working income. He harbored the belief that the home he owned would be his without fully understanding the real costs of owning an aging home. He also believed that his financial needs would somehow decrease, putting less pressure on his pension, a benefit he thought little about as it accrued through his working years. Life after retirement, he soon realized, was more expensive.

Social Security, he found, did provide him with a good check. Combined with his pension, he said, it covered his basic needs, his property taxes, and his greens fees. That, however, was all it did, he said. He was left without any extra cash. Under the Social Security rules that allow some earned income, he picked up a part-time job at a golf course pro shop. Then the economy went south, and the pro shop was forced to let its staff of part-timers go. Mick had enjoyed the contact with people of the same inclination, the prepaid greens fees, and of course, the extra money. When the job was gone, he applied for unemployment. One of the rules of unemployment insurance, however, required him to take the next job in retail that was offered him. Along came a human resources interviewer from a major northwest grocery chain, and Mick was hired.

He seems incredibly fortunate by the standards of most elderly. He has a good job with excellent insurance, adequate pay, and contact with many diverse and entertaining customers, as well as fellow employees. He may not have had a plan, but this was not how he pictured it ending.

Could seeing himself have helped him plan better? I am reminded of the Neanderthal diorama at the museum. That scene, like so many good dioramas, encompasses many different aspects of that particular moment in time. While the activities surrounding the preparation of an animal for eating take place, a hunter stands at the cave entrance, spear in hand. He looks out over an undeveloped landscape. The diorama brings the past, present, and future of the Neanderthals together in one place. You have a financial diorama, just as Mick did. You have a financial past that has brought you to this moment. You have a financial present that makes you work for a living in order to survive. Do you have a financial future that you can see? Are you the hunter who has brought back the meal but looks to the distant horizon, even with all his basic needs met?

For your financial diorama to succeed, you have to understand what you did, adjust your thinking about the present, and prepare for the future.

NIGHT SWIMMING

There is a hauntingly beautiful melody on the 1992 R.E.M. album, "Automatic for the People," entitled "Night Swimming." In it, the singer reflects on the risk and reward of taking off one's clothes at a favorite swimming hole, suggesting that in order to participate in this activity, you required only a quiet night. In the song, the words paint a vivid and poetic picture of what the future might hold when looking at the past.

Ask any 20-year-old if he thinks Social Security will be there for him when he retires, and he will answer no. Ask a 30-year-old the same question, and you will find a slight glimmer of hope that the program will be reformed, allowing her to develop a personal account that she can use to invest for herself. It would be nice if this were true, many will tell you, but they admit that the likelihood that it will be is remote—if they even gave it that much of a thought.

A 40-year-old can begin to see retirement. People in this group want to believe that the program will be there for them. They have done a little math and figure that they might just make it before the program self-destructs, as so many have predicted. They hope the minimum retirement age won't be raised again.

A 50-year-old can more or less calculate his benefits and is able to understand the role his income will play in his retirement. A 60-year-old will tell you when she can retire as well as whether she plans to continue to work to supplement the payment.

When it comes to money, and forgive me if I oversimplify this, people break down into three groups: those who have money, those who need money, and those who manage money.

People with money I often refer to as the *green class*. They tend to understand their spending limits and the power of their money. They may work, but they have earned a good deal and invested wisely, or they simply may have been born into their fortunes.

We are *blue class*. This group of people cannot be defined by the color of their collars. Wage earners in this group tend to need their paychecks. We look forward to them and budget with them. We understand money can be both comforting when we have it and devastating in its absence. If we lose a job, we eventually will be forced to make some hard financial decisions to adjust. If we have medical problems, if we have children who want to attend college, or if we have elderly parents who need care, the implications of these types of events can be life-altering. Blue-class people, those who build wealth in a paycheck-to-paycheck world, make up the majority of the people in the United States.

And then there are people like Kourtney. She was introduced to me as one of those friends of a friend who found herself at my home one afternoon last July. My wife introduced me as a financial writer. She—interest noticeably piqued—told me that she was a financial planner.

Kourtney belongs to the third group. These people are really blue-class members. They just don't want to be. Many of them admire the money they handle. They admire the wealthy people whose money they manage. Their careers and, subsequently, their own wealth reside in their ability to think rich. This belief suggests that if you understand how wealth works, you eventually can achieve the same for yourself. Understanding wealth and thinking rich have lured many people to believe that they can do simply by thinking.

Kourtney is an advisor (the new name for *stock brokers*) or planner. Her complete adoption of her clients' thinking made her a good target for a discussion of Social Security, so I baited her with the question, "What do you think about Social Security?"

But first, you need to hold that thought. A little background information about what Kourtney is strongly against should come first.

Social Security was developed as a social program to answer the growing number of families nationwide who had moved from the economies of self-sustained farming communities to the larger, industrialized cities. Social Security addressed the future of these workers when they stopped working. Without the support of the farm life, this inner-city worker was about to create a new class of poor elderly.

According to the pamphlet, "Why Social Security," published in 1934, the government explained that the money earned in a rural setting was used for luxuries rather than day-to-day expenses. The great shift from the farm to the city placed a different economic burden on both the elderly and their children. Families, who were usually small enterprises when living rurally and fending for themselves, found they had to switch to the life of a wage earner. This new way of providing a decent living meant working for money.

Workers gained rights through workers' compensation, minimum wages for public workers, and the creation in 1911 of free employment services. Lost in the shuffle, however, were the elderly. Older people needed dignity, and because of this economic shift in the American landscape, moving in with their children or helping to run the family was no longer an option.

The subject of rainy-day savings was a great concern to the authors of the publication. A recent study conducted by the Brookings Institution provided an outline of the savings habits of Americans during 1929, a year generally considered as one of our economically richest. The study showed that the top 20 percent of the earners did 98 percent of the saving. This left 80 percent of the population with only 2 percent of the nation's savings. This also meant that far too many people were seriously unprepared for life after work.

The Social Security Act of 1935 outlined benefits for old-age workers and established a retirement age. Many states had already enacted various forms of worker programs from unemployment to retirement programs within their own borders. Franklin D. Roosevelt was instrumental in implementing New York's program when he was governor of that state. When the program was proposed on a federal level during his presidency, he sought to include a "means test." A *means test* determines whether you need the additional assistance the system offers. The program began without such a test, allowing access to it by all wage earners. This created old age benefits, differing from the previous old-age assistance. Wage earners would be guaranteed a benefit when they reached age 65. This generally was accepted as the age for retirement and was close to the average life expectancy in 1930—if you survived childhood.

In January 1937, Ernest Tuckerman received a lump-sum payment from the Social Security Administration, which was slightly over a year old itself, of 17 cents. It wasn't until 3 years later that monthly benefits would begin. Ida May Fuller received that first monthly benefit check on January 31, 1940. Ms. Fuller was 65 years old when that check arrived. Because the program had only been around for 3 years, she had barely enough time to contribute to the program before she retired. The system estimated her life expectancy at about 15 years. Ida lived to be 100 years old, collecting $22,888.92 in benefits over the next 35 years on a payroll contribution of $24.75. In a message to Congress in 1934, Franklin D. Roosevelt said:

> This seeking for a greater measure of welfare and happiness does not indicate a change in values. It is rather a return to values lost in the course of our economic development and expansion.

So why has the program come under such heavy attack recently? Kourtney was able to explain this to me, which developed into a point-counterpoint type discussion.

Her opinion about retirement in general was laced with references to her father's predicament, which, in turn, became hers. Her father, a logger from southern Oregon, had come to live with her and her family recently. He had lost his job in the late nineties as companies in many small logging towns simply closed shop, citing economic hardships and the lack of available timber to process. His work stoppage, coupled with his lack of marketable skills and age, has kept him unemployed. He was the perfect example for her argument. Had he had a private account, the financial burdens he faced would have been his burden, not hers. He would have been able to keep his house. And more important, her life wouldn't have suffered the kind of disruption she is currently experiencing.

The idea of privatizing this social program cropped up several years ago at the height of the stock market boom. In an article written in 1997 for the Denver branch of the Federal Reserve, Harvey Roseblum referred to any discussion about changes to the program as being a political third rail. Touching this rail, a reference to how subway trains receive their electrical power, would cause "sudden death" to politicians who try to take on this program.

The arguments the privatizers use against the current system are well supported and well thought:

> The current program is based on a "pay as you go" basis. This was built on a formula that suggested that as long as workers exceeded retirees, there would always be a pool of funds keeping the program running. But trouble is on the horizon. The enormous amount of baby boomers, those post WW II offspring, are beginning to age and are headed straight for the program. Suddenly, people began to do the math. The ratio of workers to retirees was going to change. Under the current system, this was going to be a problem. If this happens without an increase in payroll taxes, the program would crumble under its own obligations. Currently, the company and the worker pay equal amounts to the program from each paycheck. You pay 6.2 percent; your employer contributes 6.2 percent.

We are living longer. Even current retirees are expected to live longer, putting additional and immediate pressure on the program.

Social Security may have contributed to the decline in savings. Paul Samuelson, a noted economist, once suggested that the program, because of its dependency on payroll taxes, was prohibiting savings.

Kourtney was quick to make her first point in the conversation. She works for an asset-management group for investors who do not believe in Social Security. Supposedly, this makes them a learned and wise group.

> **ME:** If we had a means test, like Roosevelt had suggested at the beginning, folks who don't need it wouldn't even be eligible. This would create a pool of saved benefits.
>
> **KOURTNEY:** So you are suggesting that wealthier income earners should contribute to the program without being able to partake in its benefits?
>
> **ME:** Absolutely. It is to their advantage to take care of the elderly through programs such as these.
>
> **KOURTNEY:** It's a pyramid scheme and should be illegal. The pro-Social Security people give everyone the impression that the program is some sort of trust account, paying folks a retirement benefit that they so justly deserve. It's not, I'm sure you know. It takes in money and immediately pays it out. The belief that your

6-plus percent contribution is being reserved for you is what keeps the program going. As long as the illusion works, the program stays up and stealing.

ME: I agree. Well, with one point you just made. It is not a retirement account. And you're right about the fact that one of the problem is people think it is.

KOURTNEY: Then it should be dismantled.

ME: Not so quick. It does a better than adequate job providing for widows and children and does give the disabled and elderly something they wouldn't otherwise have. That's a major benefit.

KOURTNEY: You think? Many of those elderly were duped into thinking that Social Security meant that they didn't have to save for retirement. Any system that relies on taxes is not only in serious need for reform. . . .

ME: I am not disagreeing on the reform issue. I am not so fond of payroll taxes either. But the idea that the plan is essentially retirement insurance for workers is misguided. It shouldn't be changed because several well-to-do investors with some investment savvy or who can afford to hire people like you have set their collective sights on any money they see as investable.

KOURTNEY: Sustaining a bankrupt system is not only foolish, it is an incredible disservice to younger workers. It might be okay for you. But for someone my age, it is something that will never pay me back what I have paid in.

ME: My age?

KOURTNEY: Your age. You are in your forties, right? Estimates that the system will be bankrupt in the next 30 years or so will only be offset by the pushing back of your retirement age. By the time you decide to call it quits, the retirement age will probably be 70.

ME: I am not treating it as a retirement plan, but I will look forward to the benefit.

KOURTNEY: The thing is, no one should be able to pick when you retire. No government agency. No regulators. Nobody. It's almost un-American. Privatization for workers who want to manage their own retirement accounts should be allowed.

(I probably should have added a description of all Kourtney's ani-
mated gestures. It was an obviously passionate topic to her, and I showed
great restraint in not "egging" her on. All she needed for that last statement was a podium.)

ME: I want to disagree.

KOURTNEY: I see something that has some sort of mechanism built in
that allows folks to siphon off only a portion of their 6.2 percent
contribution, leaving enough for a minimum amount of retirement
protection. Remember the 2000 presidential debates when Gore
and Bush duked it out over the lockbox that was Social Security
surpluses? It didn't exist. It was a neat and tidy fiction that both parties bought into. Mostly to buy votes from those blue hairs on the
take and those folks looking to begin there Floridian vacations.

Excesses collected by the 'trust fund' are immediately
lent to the Treasury. There are no real assets to make a claim
against.

ME: So you and your clients feel as though they can navigate these
markets to create real assets?

KOURTNEY: Absolutely. Right now, Social Security is the present
expressed as the future. When the program started, there were six
workers for every retiree. In a couple of decades, that ratio will
sink to two to one. Taxes will either have to skyrocket, or you
won't be kicking it on your porch until you are unable to get out
there on your own power.

ME: And you believe that the government should allow you to what,
exactly?

KOURTNEY: The current program is intergenerational. It is a promise
by this generation to pay for the past. You probably think that you
have some sort of right to those moneys.

ME: As a matter of fact, I know better. But I would be willing to bet
that the majority of folks out there believe that they do.

KOURTNEY: You would probably be right.

ME: Do you have a suggestion for fixing it?

KOURTNEY: Well, I can tell you what we shouldn't do. We shouldn't
ignore it or prop it up just because it seems like a successful pro-

gram. And we should not give the government the right to do it for us. That would open the door to making the government the coowners in public businesses.

ME: I agree with you there. Wasn't that one of the original ideas from the Clinton years?

KOURTNEY: Yeah, his administration threw that idea out for consideration. Most economists agreed that the government should stay out of the business of investing.

ME: The government can't turn away from its obligations to current and near-future retirees like me in order to give younger workers a better shot.

KOURTNEY: Have you ever done any night swimming?

ME: I grew up in the big city. Any night swimming would have been done in a backyard pool.

KOURTNEY: I grew up in southern Oregon. There was a quarry nearby that we kids swam at everyday over the summer. Even in the rain the water was cool and refreshing. But at night, the whole place changed. The water was black. The same water that you could see clearly during the day was so black and still it was like stepping into space when the sun went down. It was a challenge to go in. There was something spooky and quiet. Something risky and dangerous. Changing Social Security is like night swimming. There really isn't anything to worry about. There are lots of unknowns, I'll admit. But the water is still the same, day or night. The water is no more dangerous. It is worth the try and should be attempted.

ME: That was okay thinking when the government was running an actual surplus. But that's gone now. Wasn't there a cost for those guarantees needed to make any plan of this type workable.

KOURTNEY: Absolutely. The government will need to put up some serious cash for guarantees. Just to protect against claims. But tying individuals to their own accounts allows them to accumulate a balance that they can actually own with real property rights that can be inherited.

ME: Has it ever been done?

KOURTNEY: Yes, it has. In Chili, they privatized using index accounts, with employees paying 10 percent of their income. Employers pay nothing, although they were required to give employees an 18 percent across-the-board raise.

ME: Did it work?

KOURTNEY: Rather successfully. When people retire in Chili, their defined benefit pension, which is really what needs to be created, allowed men to retire at 65 and women to retire at 60. It isn't really privatization, though. At least not the way I think it should be run. Apparently the nation's taxpayers are still under some sort of obligation, but it is a step in the right direction.

ME: Privatization will require savings. We aren't too good at squirreling money away in this country, at least from everything I have read.

KOURTNEY: Even the Chilean experiment admitted that the change in accounting made it seem like they saved more.

ME: I am really uncomfortable with the government handling my money.

KOURTNEY: I agree. They would need to move those funds into some sort of private sector. A group that can allocate capital better.

ME: Folks like you.

KOURTNEY: Folks like me.

FLYING LESSON

My wife and I have known Berkeley and Marc for about 16 years when they purchased a great old home at the end of our street. We became fast friends. They are about 10 years younger than us and in the middle stages of child rearing. Their kids are all attending school. Berkeley hails from California, with not much in the way of family left, and Marc is from northern Maine, home to his 70-year-old parents. When we travel, they come down and collect the newspapers and mail. Their kids water our gardens. And we do the same for them. One Saturday morning we were invited to their house for a late breakfast. The invitation to dine with them aside, we knew what this really was. They were going to ply us with good food, perhaps an early afternoon coffee on the porch, and when our defenses were down, they were going to ask if we would remain executors for their estate.

Marc had gotten the urge to return to Maine to visit his parents. He had told me that this need had crept up on him rather suddenly. They were going to take an airplane, and this, we knew, was a stressful undertaking. They had thrown out a similar question 10 years ago, and we agreed. Berkeley and Marc needed to know that we would take care of their kids if anything ever happened to them.

They had never really thought about their mortality before, even when they bought life insurance. They always figured one parent would survive. But what, they asked themselves, would happen if both of them were gone? Who would care for the kids? Who would raise them in a loving home?

In Chapter 4 we talked about the necessity of some sort of off-site place for your valuables. As a renter, what you owned was in harm's way if your neighbors were careless. Important papers need safekeeping, and the cost of a safe deposit box is minimal. I also told you and will repeat, because it bears repeating, that it should be big enough to hold a video recording of your stuff. Eventually, it will be a place to put your will.

When you get to the point where you begin to plan for the future, a whole new ability is needed. Far too many Americans have no legal document stating their wishes. These people unwittingly are going to rely on their state's laws to divide their property after they pass away. This is tragic for your survivors. An attorney friend of mine speaks frequently at retirement seminars. He is an expert in labor law, and his office is legal representation for a number of labor union locals in his city. He tells me that he regularly begins his speech with a question on wills. When he queries these blue-class groups about how many in attendance have such a legal document, less than 10 percent raise their hands.

It's tough for some people to sit down and think about a time when they won't be here. The importance of having a properly written will is more than your peace of mind. It is your legacy carried forth in the manner you want. Perhaps you want your daughter to get the jewelry. You want your grandkids to get a portion of your savings for their college. You want the A.S.P.C.A. to build a new wing at the feline hospital in your name with the proceeds of your estate's sale. No one knows what those wishes are unless you put them in a legal document. These intentions are spelled out clearly in a will.

After Berkeley and Marc saw their attorney, they were sent home with the assignment of thinking through these special arrangements and naming someone to work with the attorney to help for the care of their kids. They told us that they left the office stunned at the gravity of that decision. They never thought about such a thing ever happening. They would always be there for their kids. Now they were faced with the possibility of thinking about a time when they wouldn't.

To make a long story short, we did agree. Breakfast was a revisiting of that decision and a renewal of that agreement. Marc's urge to return to see his parents was putting pressure on Berkeley. Wills make you think about the worst. They force you to decide about the division of your property and how you want your kids cared for. This forward thinking provides you with the feeling that the loose ends are tied up. It is a strange and rare feeling of completeness.

As your estate grows in size (over time, this usually happens, sometimes without you even realizing it), you should review how you want your "things" dispersed. I am reminded of two stories when it comes to estate planning. The first involves Berkeley's mother, who revised the executor of her will on a weekly basis. You could tell, based on the dates, which child was in favor at the moment. At the time of her death, Berkeley's brother was the favored one, and the task of taking care of the estate fell to him.

The other story involves the man who wanted to take all his money with him. His will made it explicit that he wanted to be buried with his wealth. When the widow was asked at the funeral whether she had complied with the deceased's wishes, she said she had. She put a check in the coffin.

Wills in most states are simple documents that outline your wishes for the disposal of your property. Your attorney retains a copy, and you are given one for your safe deposit box. In many states, when the spouse dies, the estate automatically goes to the surviving spouse. If both spouses die and there is no will, the property goes into what is called *probate court*. The judge can decide on a good many things, including satisfying your debts and taxes and determining who gets whatever is left. This can be a difficult time for your survivors, who may have thought that you would have wished them to possess certain objects of sentimentality. All estates go to probate; only those without wills remain there.

The soul searching involved in writing a will requires you to look at your future in a way that you probably have not done before. You look at where you would like your family to be in your absence.

Most people find it easy to skirt this issue as long as possible. But no matter when you do it, the importance of doing it can't be ignored for long. Let the last and final document outline your wishes, and do as Berkeley and Marc have done—revisit it occasionally.

If you are married, estate taxes should be considered. It is amazing how quickly our real worth can change. Retirement plans, the appreciated value of your home, and your insurance policies can make your survivors suddenly wealthy. A review of where you are financially, done every couple of years, will keep your heirs out of any tax trouble. Currently, a married couple's estate is excluded from tax when the value of that estate falls below $1,350,000. An individual can pass on $675,000 without penalty to his or her heirs. Future tax reforms can change those figures, so check with your attorney.

You always should consult an attorney in these matters. Attorneys do know best. If your fortune should change, revisit them to ward off the potential of tax problems.

There are, of course, two things you can do prior to growing your estate. Married couples should label joint property as *joint tenants*. This saves some probate questions and possibly a few dollars in legal fees.

And second, be sure that your life insurance policy is irrevocable. Such a policy is kept outside the estate when considering value. This can help with the payment of any taxes that may have forced the sale of some assets, and it gives the family some cash to help settle those problems. If you have ever been involved in the settlement of an estate, you will know what I mean.

If you haven't, don't be so quick to accept what Berkeley and Marc have asked of my wife and me. Assuming the responsibility of executor is no easy job—especially if there are kids involved. We knew this couple very well. We knew that they have built a good financial structure for themselves and their kids. Doing this while you are alive and healthy makes it easier for those who are left to take care of your business.

How do you find a good attorney? If you belong to a trade association, consult with it. Friends and neighbors are also good places to go for recommendations. But remember to go prepared. Have your estate in line, your assets and insurance policies, mutual fund statements, and tax information listed for their perusal. The first and only rule of thumb for dealing with an attorney is "Time is your money."

THE ATTRACTION OF FISHING

Or golf, traveling, spoiling grandchildren, moving to a sunny, warm location, or doing volunteer work—the attraction is how intoxicating those dreams are. But what exactly is retirement?

Retirement has become synonymous with money. To comprehend retirement, it is more important to understand that the age of retirement isn't as important as the "how you retire," and it requires a plan.

The next four chapters in this book will concern themselves in one way or another with your retirement from a financial point of view. But this is only a part of the puzzle. This puzzle will be based on an ever-shifting wave of good and bad fortune, earned and lost wealth and opportunities, and good old-fashioned fate.

So how do you know what you want from retirement? This is an excellent question with no single answer. My wife and I agree that retirement means simply working in absence of a clock. Without time harnessing the day, work would seem much more pleasurable and effortless. We both plan on remaining active, convinced that it is good not only for our physical health but also for our mental well-being.

The first criterion of how you plan on retiring should be your health. That part of the plan should begin now. The last thing a moderate financial plan can handle is long-term illnesses. Some are unavoidable and may even be genetic. Take some measure to include these possible problems in your plan. Making a move toward better health while you are still formulating or building your plan can be a key to its success.

The second criterion for a good plan is jokingly referred to around our house as the "past benefit-redemption plan." This requires only two things: children and cultivating them to be able to take care of you in an emergency. We rib our children, suggesting that the only reason we are being nice to them now is based on the possibility that they will take care of us in the future. Plans are not without flaws. And unfortunately, most of those flaws are unforeseen. In truth, neither my wife nor I want to spend our golden years with our kids and their families. A good plan will ensure that that will be a last possible option.

The third and necessary piece to the plan is your belief that what you are shooting for is attainable. If you are looking to live better than you are living now, you had better be prepared to make some sacrifices now to get there.

My wife and I have been preparing our home for our retirement for the last 8 years. Major repairs have been completed, and upgrades have made this a difficult space to replace. We like the area and the long-term chances that it will only improve. On the other hand, those improvements will reward us handsomely should we ever need to sell or reverse-mortgage the property, a financial trick for those who are real estate rich and cash poor.

How much is enough? I wrote a while back, in my conversation with Kourtney, that we are not depending on Social Security benefits, but we will enjoy them nonetheless. Our plan has us living in a paid-for home, working at something but not doing what we have done most of our lives, collecting from my pension and our retirement plans, and using the Social Security benefit to finance madcap adventures.

We have no idea, with a good many viable working years ahead of us, whether this is feasible, but we definitely think that it is attainable. Property taxes will be a consideration, but we believe that we have built in some leeway in our plan. We can always cut the madcap adventures down to an occasional visit to the grandkids. We have no doubt that inflation will play some roll in our plans as well. What that will be, we hope will be minimal. Over the last two decades, inflation has been kept in close check. Rising prices in the grocery store and for home heating also could keep us counting pennies in our old age.

Planning for these problems, whose face value is unknown, is not only cautious but wise as well. Finding the exact cost of these is next to impossible. Financial planners claim to have the solution for these problems. They don't. These plans are only as good as your participation and commitment.

Some of you may view this as shooting fairly low in the expectation department. I disagree. My wife and I have arrived at our future vision while we are still in our thirties and early forties. We still had kids. The end looked incredibly far off, and fortunately, we think that distance is still quite far away. We keep trying things that we think we might like to do when we retire. "This is what it will be like," she will turn to me and say. Yes, I agree, retirement with her will be very nice indeed.

Retirement should mean what Izaak Walton suggested it should be in his book, *The Compleat Angler.* Written in seventeenth-century England, the book illustrates Walton's love for fishing and suggests that the path to salvation is clear if it is in the pursuit of pleasure. We understood that to get to retirement with our sanity in tact, we need to lower our sights, understand our expectations, and not sacrifice the daily pleasures of life in too great an abundance.

DRAWING CONCLUSIONS

As we learned from Mick, a good plan started early will keep retirement surprises to a minimum. While the chance to work can be both healthy and profitable, the work should be optional. Begin to explore your future as early as possible.

- Social Security is in need of some sort of reform. The unfortunate consequence is the simple fact that you will need to take some sort of active participation in your own retirement planning. Relying on this program for your retirement may prove to be foolhardy.
- You shouldn't wait until you are about to take a trip to get a will. If you have children, a sizable estate, or are a partner in a business, this legal document can keep your survivors from unnecessary hardship.
- Although your attorney should mention this, all your documents in which you need to have a beneficiary named, such as insurance

policies and retirement accounts, should read "as per will" and should be stored in a safe deposit box. Your attorney will keep a copy as well. This document should be updated every 5 years or so unless your fortunes change or you are, like Berkeley and Marc, about to take a long journey.

7

Step 7: Buy Bonds—The Blander, the Better

My concept of what a bond investor is has changed little over the years. Before I knew Sam's name, he was introduced to me as "the Professor."

Bond investors, by the nature of the investment itself, need to be both experienced and knowledgeable. The Professor had a wry wit with liberal doses of mischief thrown in, as well as the notable trait of self-mockery. These characteristics also should be the possessions of a bond investor. If you can't laugh a little at yourself, be generally critical, and be ever so much the child, you will have difficulty embracing the odd nature of bonds.

I saw the Professor every Saturday for 10 years. He was cordial and never seemed like he wanted to speak for long. Our relationship was based on the telling of an off-colored joke, the uncomfortable laughter that followed, and a question about how my investments were doing in the market. Once a private subject among good and close friends, discussing your investments in the open seemed to have become much more commonplace in the middle to late 1990s. Folks would boast about this Internet company with this or that new product. Everyone was making money. Everyone seemed to be sharing his or her expertise with each other. There was, it seemed, enough to go around.

Sam, who, truth be told, wasn't a professor at all, taught history at a community college until his retirement. Since then, he has tinkered with his hobbies and invested in bonds, a passion that fits my picture of what a bond investor looks like.

TIED TOGETHER

It's time for a short economics lesson. Bond investors are the antistock investors. However, the two are tied together at the wrist, although at first glance it doesn't seem possible.

When the stock market goes up, investors run away from bonds. When the stock market is in trouble, investors run to bonds. Both events are tied to the economy, and the economy is tied to business. The first 3 years of this decade have seen the bond market surge as the stock market has struggled out of doldrums that seemed to never end. As the economy begins to rebound, the stock market will surge, and the bond market will suffer.

The health of the economy depends on the financial health of its participants. If companies are growing, they hire folks to come and produce their products. The wages produced as a result of these jobs keep other parts of the economy growing as spending increases. This raises the tax base of local, state, and federal governments, and the whole of these parts becomes a simplistic explanation of what an economy is. The combination is essential.

Companies prefer to use the stock market to raise money. It is a more efficient method that creates ownership for the holder of a share. However, when the face value of that piece of paper (a share), determined by the open marketplace, is not what you or the company values it to be, the stock market is no longer as efficient. This doesn't stop the company's need for money, however.

Without the use of stock as currency, companies turn to issuing debt or, to put it another way, issuing bonds. Bondholders are lenders. They understand that every company, government, or municipality needs money, and they are willing to lend their money to these organizations, provided they are paid back with interest.

Earlier in this book I spoke about the value of a good credit rating. A good credit rating helps to determine the interest rate you get when you borrow. When you buy bonds, the roll is reversed. You are the one who, by purchasing a bond, demands proof of credit. You have become the lender. You will determine the creditworthiness of the company, government, or municipality and lend your money accordingly. You ask yourself, the same as any lender would, the following questions: Is the borrower a good risk? Can the borrower afford the loan? Can the borrower pay me back? You have money to lend, and the borrower needs money. All that is left is the terms.

This country's central bank, the Federal Reserve Bank, attempts to shape the economy using interest rates and monetary policy. The interest rate, which incidentally has little to do with mortgage rates, is the overnight rate available to the nation's biggest banks. Monetary policy is simply having just the right amount of money circulating to keep the economy running. This is the very stripped-down explanation.

Bonds are affected by these actions. Bond investors closely watch both interest rates and monetary policy. As lenders, bondholders are looking for companies, governments, or municipalities that are willing to borrow money at high rates.

The Federal Reserve Bank lowers interest rates to stimulate growth. If money is inexpensive to borrow, companies will use it to build factories, and that, in turn, will grow jobs. Bondholders would prefer higher rates. Thus, as we move on, you know two things: Bonds are essentially loans, and interest rates affect them.

Bonds are far from risk-free. The effect of interest rates can compromise your investment. When buying a bond, it is extremely important that you determine the interest-rate sensitivity.

This sensitivity is based on duration. This new term, *duration,* deals with the length of the bond. For instance, if you were to purchase a 30-year Treasury note, the duration would be 30 years. You are giving the federal government 30 years to pay you back with interest. If you are giving Ford Motor Company 5 years to pay you back, the duration will be 5 years.

Bond Types

Taxable Bond Funds	Duration
Short	0 to 3.5 years
Intermediate	3.5 to 6 years
Long	6+ years
Tax-Exempt Bond Funds	**Duration**
Short	0 to 4.5 years
Intermediate	4.5 to 7 years
Long	7+ years

Another consideration in the purchase of a bond deals with its creditworthiness. Here is where you will need help. A credit agency such as Moody's or Standard & Poor's issues ratings on bonds. The higher the rating, the greater is the chance that you will be repaid in full. The lower the rating, the greater is the chance that your money will be lost if the company defaults on the bond or goes under. Bondholders, though, can stand in line at a bankruptcy proceeding with their hands extended looking to be paid back. This is one of the biggest differences between bonds and stocks. You are not an owner in the company the way a shareholder is. You are a lender, and you are entitled to be paid. Shareholders aren't.

Moody's rates long-term bonds based on creditworthiness as follows:

Aaa. This is the best-quality bond with the smallest degree of investment risk and the highest rated, are as safe as stuffing the money you invested under the mattress.

Aa. Not much of a notch down, having the same high quality by all standards, we can refer to as high grade.

A. These bonds may possess many of the same favorable investment attributes but are not as high quality. Whatever the issues these bonds have with the credit ratings, they are still considered as upper- to medium-grade obligations.

Baa. These bonds are secured with what the credit folks call medium-grade obligations. These obligations are not as well supported and are considered riskier. Whatever is being used as security is not as highly rated or as well secured as lenders (bond buyers) would like. Bonds rated Baa and above are considered investment-grade bonds.

Ba. As the ratings decline, so do does the faith in the ability of these companies or governments to repay the debt. The risk increases substantially. But so does the reward. These types of bonds have what are called *speculative elements.* This translates into "problematic future." So bonds with ratings of Ba and below are generally considered speculative.

B. These low-rated bonds are bordering on gambling. The issuers of these bonds are not likely to make good on their end of the bargain, and the buyer of these bonds should understand the risk. Bonds with this rating are not considered a desirable investment.

Caa. Close to worth ignoring, these and bonds rated lower are considered by investors to be junk. These bonds are riddled with problems and are not recommended for the average investor.

C. Almost off the chart, these bonds, rated the lowest, have extremely poor prospects of ever attaining any real investment standing.

To this list of considerations when buying a bond investment, you can add: Bonds are essentially loans, and interest rates affect them. Moreover, duration and creditworthiness can add or subtract from the potential risk.

Bonds can be purchased in one of two ways—either individually, as the Professor preferred, or as part of a mutual fund. In a mutual fund, the managers do their best at juggling the maturity dates of the bonds they hold. The *maturity date* is the pay-up time for the borrower. When you buy bonds on an individual basis, there is a little trick you can use to keep your money always in peak form—laddering.

Laddering is a proven style for this type of investment. The principle is simple: When dealing with investments such as bonds, the goal is to keep your money continually invested. To do that, you would buy bonds with different maturity dates, often based on 2-year increments. The idea of keeping your money actively invested saves you from interest-rate fluctuations. By owning bonds with maturity dates of 2, 4, 6, 8, and 10 years, you can spread out the selling and reinvesting. For example, when a 2-year bond matures in your portfolio, you use the net receipts to purchase a new 10-year bond. In a well-laddered portfolio, the bondholder will have bonds with different durations. A bond that is coming due will be used to purchase a new 10-year note. Interest rates vary over long periods of time. Laddering protects the investor from having to reinvest when rates are less favorable.

Laddering is very complicated. This investment style comes with many pitfalls for the average individual investor. Not only is there the consideration and tracking of credit risk, as well as the possibility that the company will default on its obligation (the risk of not getting back what you loaned them), there is also the possibility that the bond comes with call provisions in place. *Call provisions* act like a home refinance for the borrower. They pay off the original obligation using a bond with lower interest payments. A call provision slaughters your long-term return by paying you early. Not only does this reduce the return, but you are also forced to find someplace else to put your money—with any luck, at the same rate of return as the bond that was just called.

Buying individual bonds does not always net you the best price. Add to this the bother of laddering, a seemingly endless task, and you have an investment that seems custom made for old men with cynical natures and a good deal of time to waste. Individual bonds are work.

Put that bond in a bond fund, and you have a beast of a much tamer nature. Bond funds provide the blue-class investor with the right amount of sophistication for the less sophisticated among us. The best way to create a fixed-income environment with a predetermined amount of risk is to invest in a bond fund.

Bond funds, however, are not bonds. The Professor shunned bond funds in favor of individual issues. Bonds bought individually sometimes come with coupons. Coupons are monthly, quarterly, or annual payments made by the borrower to you. The professor's bond investments give him extra spending money on a regular and consistent basis.

Bond funds, on the other hand, provide the investor with diversification by investing in many different types of bonds with varying durations, yields, and returns. What such funds lack, however, are the guarantees of a monthly check from coupons and principal. These are generally reinvested in the fund, growing the value of the overall investment. Bond funds collect the value of the portfolio, do some quick arithmetic, and determine what is called the *net asset value* (NAV). When you buy into a bond fund, this determines the share price. Because this price can change, the value of your principal can as well. The NAV, by regulation, must be calculated at the end of the day's business. With individual bonds, there is no risk that principal can be lost due to a falling NAV.

Bond funds do, however, come with certain costs that are present in all mutual-investing situations. Someone has to run the fund. The manager or management team is involved in the day-to-day running of the business. One of the problems true bond investors have with bond funds is something called *transparency*. Lack of transparency in the fund's holdings, or the inability to have access to full disclosure, makes truly sophisticated investors turn their collective noses up at bond funds. The good news is that the downside to bond fund investing more or less stops right there.

The upside far outweighs the downside. Professionally managed bond funds provide individual investors with the opportunity to grow their money in a safe haven. Fund managers not only are able to buy bonds at a better rate than individuals can, but their research into call provisions and creditworthiness also far exceeds that of the average investor. Pricing structure is very important to the success of a bond fund. Bond prices are set at a percentage of their redemption value. This is called *par*, and the value is set at 100. An individual may buy a bond for an eighth or a quarter point below par and believe that she has received a good price. The bond fund manager may buy that same bond for 4 percent below par.

This is, in essence, how fund managers justify their fees. The spread they receive usually offsets any fees they may charge to manage the fund. Fund managers often tout their ability to be flexible. Bonds are not stationary investments. Managers can keep your money in a very active state with a good deal of buying and selling.

I mentioned, as did the Professor in one conversation I recall, that interest-rate fluctuations are murderous on an individual investor's attempt at laddering. The par value can work against an individual. Selling at maturity leaves you with little in the way of repurchasing options if the only bonds available are yielding less than the bond you just sold. The skill of a bond investor lies mostly in his ability to get good par value. A repurchase schedule doesn't take into consideration par value. Fund managers can look for opportunities in between those maturity dates, outpacing an individual's ability to do as well.

Fund managers are more in tune to the possibility of callable bonds, the ones whose issuers can redeem and then reissue their bonds at lower interest rates. Individuals who invest in bonds often will take this possibility into consideration and avoid these types of provisions. This strategy, however, passes over some great opportunities.

One of the most confusing structures in bonds is the relation between price and yield. When the price of a bond goes up, the yield, or the amount of interest you receive, goes down. When the yield is high, the price of the bond is low. The Professor, in one of his longest conversations, explained how bond pricing works. Every borrower wants to attract a lender. In order to attract these lenders, he explained, the borrower offers a bond with a face value, duration, and fixed amount of interest.

"For the sake of round numbers, let's say the bond is worth $1000. The borrower wants to pay the loan back in 2 years and will pay the lender 6 percent in interest. This bond has a face value or principal of $1000, a duration of 2 years, and a yield of 6 percent. Every year the bondholder will receive $60. At the end of 2 years, the lender will receive his $1000 back." That, he said, was the simple explanation.

His tutorial continued: "Suppose that the economy gets worse. When that happens, interest rates on the open market tend to go down. That's when the Fed steps in and tries to keep money cheap to borrow. That works against you, the lender. The borrower now has lenders competing for his business. He can offer the same bond for less interest or at a lower yield. This makes the bond with the higher interest payment more attractive.

"The bondholder with the 6 percent bond knows that his bond is now worth more, so he decides to sell his note. Because of the higher yield on his note, he raises the price. The $1000 face value has risen, causing the yield to drop."

Just so I understood, I repeated what he said. The bond is worth more, so the owner of the $1000 bond receives more for the bond with the higher yield. "And that," he said, "pushes the real return of the bond lower."

Frankly, I was thrilled with the amount of time he was spending with me. Unused to these long lectures, I pushed him for the opposite possibility, a good economy. He continued with this brief explanation.

"Good economies tend to do the exact opposite. A bond issued before the economy improved will have a lower yield than current issues." And with that, he walked away. Good economic times produce low prices. Bond prices are lower when there are many bonds for sale. In order to attract buyers, the yields go up. When the economy is bad, bond prices go up because the need to borrow from the bond market is higher, with no need to pay those customers high yields to keep their business.

Once we grasp the movements of price and yield and what they mean to each other—how when one is up, the other is down—the question that begs to be asked is, How do you determine which to look at when buying a bond fund? If you look at a bond fund's 12-month average, there is a good possibility that the yield will reflect a variety of income-producing bonds, each with a different yield. These yields are averaged. A 12-month moving average of 15 percent actually might produce less income because of a portfolio containing many different yielding bonds. According to some experts in the field, the 30-day moving average is a better indication of income and performance.

In each instance, the effects of time play a significant role in whether you make any real money. Some bond funds will show you little in the way of profit despite reinvested dividends if you sell too soon. Buying a bond fund when the economy is in poor shape will net you a fund full of high-priced, low-yield bonds. Buying that same fund in an improved economy will give you higher-yield, lower-priced bonds. Because of the varying durations of the bonds such funds hold, the long-term approach is by far the best method for investing in bond funds. Allowing your money to ride out bad spells and earn substantially in good times gives you the performance you seek.

Over the years, I have received numerous e-mails through my Web site asking about bonds. Below are some of the best of those questions:

Question: Are bonds and bond funds traded on the New York Stock Exchange (NYSE)? When you go to your broker and ask her to buy shares in a bond fund, where does she go to purchase those shares?

Answer: No, bonds are not traded on the NYSE, the NASDAQ, or any other board that trades equities (stocks). You can purchase bonds and bond funds through a broker or directly from the issuers of those bonds (such as the government) and from the companies who manage those bond funds. A great many mutual fund families have these types of funds. Some companies sell nothing but bond funds.

Question: Who regulates bond funds? Is it the Securities and Exchange Commission (SEC)? Can this regulatory body suspend trading on a fund that is suspect?

Answer: You should understand what a bond is first. A company, municipality, or government issues bonds in an effort to raise money for projects or purchases. The SEC is concerned with how a company operates. The SEC regulates companies that issue bonds, protecting you from fraud. In order to attract investors to purchase these bonds, the issuing entity is often rated by outside companies such as Moody's or Standard & Poor's that determine the quality of the debt. If the debt issued is based on rock-solid ground (such as the U.S. government, who has never defaulted on a bond payment), the bond receives a high rating such as AAA. As the risk increases, the rating deteriorates in tandem. As the risk increases, so does the opportunity for the investor to make money. This is expressed as yield. To better understand this, when the yield is high, the price is low. The higher the price, the lower is the yield.

When we look at these ratings, those with the highest risk are the ones most likely not to pay investors what they have coming. In other words, the riskier the bond or bond fund, the greater is the reward if everything goes well. These bonds are sometimes referred to as *junk*. A much more attractive name is *high-yield*. Either way, you are taking a chance.

Question: Can your bonds or bond funds collapse?

Answer: Bond funds do not necessarily collapse. Bonds, however, can default. This means that they cannot pay their debt, and the company is usually headed toward bankruptcy or reorganization. If a bond fund is holding some of these very risky investments, you will feel the damage as well but on a smaller scale. Bond funds spread your risk among many bonds. Some of the most recent failures include companies such as Enron and Worldcom. The emphasis during the collapse of these companies was on the plummeting share price. Many investors in the stock of these companies lost everything. While bondholders took a serious hit as well, they were awarded some compensation because they held the debt of the company.

Question: When a bond fund fails, does some entity regulate what the shareholders get back? Or must shareholders try to sell their bond fund holdings for whatever they can get in the open market-place?

Answer: No, bondholders are not shareholders, except in a bond fund. Bond funds usually don't fail. Bond fund investors need to be aware that some bonds are also fraught with great risk. Risk is, in essence, your willingness to take a gamble with your money. A company with a low credit rating issuing a high-yield bond is a risk. These types of bonds produce eye-popping returns, but not without great skill (and guts) by the bond manager or the individual investor.

Bonds break down into just a few groups. From there, they get plenty complicated. There are the U.S. government–backed securities. These include the *Treasury bonds* or *notes* that you hear the most about. The new benchmark of this group is a bond whose duration is 10 years to maturity. This is the bond those zany-jacketed traders in the bond pits in Chicago use to set interest rates for mortgages. I'd be willing to bet that you thought mortgage rates had something to do with the interest rate published by the Federal Reserve.

In the case of Treasury bonds, you are lending money to the government. The government, in return, offers you safety backed by the "full faith and credit" of the federal government. In other words, the government has always paid up. Your principal and interest are guaranteed. These bonds can be affected by other factors, however, and they are difficult to predict over long periods. The influential factors are inflation and interest rates.

Inflation is the result of rising prices. The Federal Reserve largely controls inflation to some degree through interest rates. Raising rates helps to keep inflation in check but plays havoc with bond investments. The Treasury has a solution for the inflation effect—*Treasury inflation-protected securities* (TIPS) are bonds that are protected from this type of risk against your return. Understanding the way inflation can erode the value of a bond, the Treasury began offering this product, whose interest is based on the consumer price index (CPI) published by the Bureau of Labor Statistics. The way it works is unique to this type of bond. When you buy a TIPS bond for $1000, the erosion that inflation causes is taken into account. This bond, based on a 10-year inflation index, for the sake of using round numbers, is paying you 5 percent. You always will be guaranteed to receive at least 5 percent. This will be calculated and paid to you every 6 months, a half at a time. On your $1000 investment, you can expect a payment of $25.

Suppose, however, that inflation has begun to accelerate. The CPI has moved up, and this means that your principal will go up by that amount. Once again, for the sake of simplicity, suppose that inflation has gone up from 1 to 6 percent. This is added to your principal. In other words, the value of your $1000 has just increased, making it worth what it originally was worth. Now, when your interest is calculated, it is against the new value of your bond.

The math works something like this:

$$\$1000 \times 1\% = \$1010$$

The new calculation of your principal against interest looks like this:

$1010 (the inflation-adjusted value) × 5% (the interest rate) =

$$\$50.50 \div 2 \text{ (once every 6 months)} = \$25.25$$

Savings bonds, those popular gifts for children, also can be an excellent low-cost way to save under the umbrella of safety. These Series EE bonds are bought, usually directly from a Federal Reserve bank, in a wide variety of denominations from $50 on up to $10,000. These bonds are purchased for half the face value (a $50 bond costs $25). Hold on to it for 17 years, and you can redeem them for full value. You also can hold them for an additional 13 years, collecting more interest. Series I bonds have a built-in inflation index. Both these bonds are tax-deferred, meaning that you receive no income until you actually cash the bond in. If you use the money for higher education, these types of savings bonds even may be tax-deductible.

On a much more local level, states, cities, and counties issue the same type of offer called *municipal bonds*. The money raised usually is borrowed from citizens for special projects such as building a library or repairing roads and bridges. The locality offers its bonds in much the same way the U.S. government does. Such bonds offer current income that sometimes is free not only of federal taxes but also of state and local taxes as well. Such bonds, for the most part, are rated highly for safety. In other words, you stand a better than excellent chance of getting your principal back, paid in full. Municipal bonds come in all sorts of varieties to suit almost every investor's horizon, risk tolerance, and type. They also are easy to sell because of these factors. And lastly, the income is something you can count on.

A federal law making municipal bonds tax-free enhanced their attractiveness. In many instances, the state won't tax you either for the generous offer of your funds. Tax-exempt can mean a lot.

From our previous example using TIPS, let's suppose that the $1000 was used to buy a municipal bond from Nicetown, U.S.A. The town is going to use the money for improvements to its sewer lines. The going rate for the issue is 5.0 percent. But you are torn. You can get a much better rate with a taxable bond for the same face value paying 7.5 percent. How do you choose?

	Tax-Exempt	Taxable
Investment	$1000	$1000.00
Interest	$50	$75.00
Income tax @ 35%	0	$26.25
New return	$50	$48.75
Yield	5%	4.9%

I have thrown the word *yield* about quite liberally in the last couple of pages. Now it's time for a review. *Yield* is the total amount or return on your investment should you hold the bond until it matures. In the tax-exempt example, the yield is expressed as *yield to maturity* because the cost of taxes does not affect the return.

Municipal bonds are not always tax-exempt. *General bonds,* usually voter-approved, are paid by tax receipts. *Revenue bonds* are paid for by tolls or charges or even by rent payments. The federal government approves these two types of bonds for tax-exempt status. If you want to borrow money to build that new baseball stadium, the bond issued in that instance is not tax-exempt.

To attract investors away from the safety of government or municipal bonds, companies have had to offer higher yields when selling their *corporate bonds.* They offer a wider range of opportunities to make (and to lose) you money. These bonds come with risk that is based on the quality of the company and what it needs the money to do.

Corporate bonds break down three ways. *Registered bonds* come with your name on them. The company knows who you are and sends you your payment at regular intervals; when the bond matures, the company sends you back your money. *Bearer bonds* have coupons attached and no name on them. The Tax Reform Act of 1982 eliminated this type of bond, but there are still quite a lot in circulation. The holder of a bearer bond simply can redeem the coupon attached to the bond for a cash payment of interest. In Dan Brown's novel, *The DaVinci Code,* a bishop is paid in Vatican bearer bonds. When the bonds are offered to a taxi driver as payment, the driver, misunderstanding what they are, chooses to take the bishop's amethyst and diamond ring instead. A *book bond* is held by your broker or by your mutual fund manager. Although you own it, your name never actually appears on the bond.

A necessary component in the diversification of your bond investments, corporate bonds should be purchased through bond funds. Corporate bonds can range from conservative to risky depending on the quality of the company that issues them.

This is why a good money manager is important. Far be it from me to say that bond investing is more difficult than equity investing, but I will. Equity investors seem more emotionally charged. Bond investors look for angst. They *want* to worry.

Bonds are an important part of a diverse portfolio, and if you are still working, corporate bonds and, even more preferably, corporate bond funds should play a role in your retirement plan. How much of a role? This, as always, depends on who you are, not on how old you are. If you are starting out late and this book finds itself in the hands of someone who has done little in the way of saving for retirement, then buy only high-yield bond funds with good 5-year returns. A good high-quality fund with a skillful manager at the helm can provide a decent return, usually well above other bond funds. This could do wonders for a cautious investor with not much tucked away. No more than a third of your investments should be bonds, no matter how cautious you are. Bond funds are part of a diversified portfolio.

Suppose, however, that you are young, just starting out. Then the only conservative investment in your portfolio should be a balanced fund. These funds invest in a blend of stocks and bonds and are hard to benchmark. *Benchmarking* is a method of comparing your fund with an average or similar investment, usually an index of a group. I will say more about this later.

However, if you are almost retired or can see the chances of leaving your job for good increasing daily, corporate bond funds should play a considerable role in your planning. There are other kinds of bond funds, and I will get to them in a moment, but I want to stress the importance of some risk in your plans. A corporate bond fund run by a good manager with a good track record and low fees is essential to a good plan. Gauging your risk is quite another thing, but in many cases your risk is greatly diminished by investing in a fund. Please note: Your risk is diminished *not eliminated.* There is always the chance that you can lose your investment, but such chances are greatly reduced in a good bond fund.

Many of the bond funds listed below also will give you the duration as a way to describe what they do. The shorter the time frame, the higher is the quality of the debt. For instance, the *ultra-short-term bond funds* are designed to provide a better than money market return without any real added risk. Morningstar.com has reported on these funds, saying, "the average ultra short bond fund has not lost money over any trailing 12-month period" since the company initiated tracking 20 years ago. Such funds are able to outgain taxable money market funds by investing in the highest-grade bonds, usually rated AAA, which keeps them a very conservative investment indeed.

Long-term government bond funds are the funds to which investors run when the world of investing looks like a scary place. Corporate scandals, poor overall economic performance, and the uncertainty of the world in general are when these bonds are at their most attractive.

Long-term corporate bond funds are always facing the risk that interest rates won't cooperate (low interest rates mean that in order to attract investors, they must offer higher rates of return) and that the bonds they are holding can be called using the call provision we discussed earlier or simply by the company defaulting on its obligation. The upside is a better than average return for the investor, though.

Bond funds that use a combination of mortgage income, corporate bonds, and inflation-indexed Treasuries are usually called *intermediate-term corporate bond funds*. These are very diverse funds with bond holdings that are sensitive to interest rates. When rates are low, corporate bonds tend to underperform, whereas the mortgage income and TIPS in such funds do better. Should interest rates rise, the funds use the corporate holdings to balance in the other direction. The way these bonds are structured, they provide protection from almost any market setback.

Short-term corporate bond funds are not free of risk. The longer the duration, the better is the return; the shorter the duration, the smaller is the return. This means that the best short-term bond funds need not only the perfect mix of interest-sensitive corporate bonds but also a knack for active and nimble management.

High-yield bond funds invest in companies whose creditworthiness is in question. While this does not pose too great a risk for a bond fund investor, the risk is still there. You are rewarded for this, however, in the form of greater returns. Equity investors running from markets that aren't doing well like the returns these types of funds deliver.

DRAWING CONCLUSIONS

Bonds are essentially loans, and interest rates can and will affect them. Duration and creditworthiness can add to or subtract from the potential risk. Typically, bond funds are better investments because of their flexibility and because they are able to get better prices, tend to have better research departments than the individual has access to, and can sell these services at a reasonable cost. It also should be noted that inflation has an impact, especially on longer-term bonds, and likewise, taxes should be taken into consideration. All of these factors can affect your yield.

- As we move through these last chapters of the book, the word *allocation* will start to crop up. Allocation is just a fancy word for share or portion. Good investors divide their portfolios up into different categories in order to spread the risk. Spreading the risk helps your portfolio in two ways. First, it allows you to continue to grow your money if one particular investment is doing poorly.

Second, it allows you to concentrate on enjoying yourself and not worrying about the performance of your plan. Long-term strategies extend far beyond the time when we retire. We are planning to live a long time, and our investments should be thought of in much the same manner. Bond funds should be a part of everyone's plan.

- The best bond fund tends to be expensive, meaning that many have fees either up front (open-ended) or at the end (closed-ended) or, worse, demand enormous amounts of money to invest. Find a fund that charges you nothing to invest. This is called *no-load.* Then narrow your search—and the Internet is an excellent place to do this—to funds that have low fees. These fees are the ones the management charges to run the fund. Then look for *tenure,* or the time the manager or the management team has been with the fund. Five years is a good minimum. More than that is even better. Then look at the return over that period. A bond manager has seen a lot over that time from a great market in bonds to a bad market. The return will be a good indication of the future return you are likely to receive. Time and space do not allow me to list all the different types of bond funds available to the average investor. If you follow some of the basic investment rules noted earlier, you should be able to navigate these waters just fine. Please read the prospectus that comes with the fund, and always ask questions if you do not understand. This is a good blue-class rule of thumb.

- I found out several months ago that Sam, the Professor, had passed away after a short illness. Always one to keep people at arm's length, his absence left those who knew him wondering where he was. When he died, he took with him a treasure of insights into the world of fixed-income investing. He will be missed.

8

Step 8: Play the Market

I have a little story for you. There were three travelers on a train. One was an investor, another was an analyst, and the third was an economist.

This train speeds by what looks like a black sheep standing in profile, and the conversation of the three passengers immediately turns to what they had just seen. The investor reaches the conclusion that all sheep are black. He saw a black sheep, and therefore, in his experience, this is a good assumption. The analyst understands that there is more than one explanation, and being analytical, she suggests that some sheep are black. The economist arrives at the conclusion that there is not enough information available at first glance. He instead points out the existence of at least one sheep and that at least one-half of that sheep is black.

I felt that this story was worth telling for two reasons. We all tend to be investors too often, analysts only when it suits us, and almost never do we shy away from the promise of riches when clearly we should simply know better.

The second reason is that the approach we take to investing is often seeded with outlandish hopes. Investing is a slow and methodical process that needs time and patience to unfold.

The next step in this "bottoms up" approach introduces you to the rewards of a little-heralded investment that can act to salve both your craving for the stock market and the best attributes of real estate investing.

OWNING AMERICA

Mamiko is one of those hard-working immigrants you read about. She came to America 10 years ago, the daughter of a fish merchant from a small village on Japan's northern coast. Through a program sponsored by a restaurant, Mamiko came to the United States. She worked in the kitchen, saving her money. She eventually opened her own sushi parlor and then began to teach the art on a full-time basis. Her work was her life, and she found herself living a sparse existence with few trappings. Her grandfather had always told her growing up that once in America, she should own land.

She was troubled. She had no time for land, as her grandfather had wished for her. She confided her situation to a friend, who, as good fortune would have it, recently added a REIT indexed mutual fund to her portfolio. Mamiko had no idea what her friend was talking about, but the crude definition her friend provided her piqued Mamiko's interest.

A *real estate investment trust* (*REIT*), Mamiko was soon to discover, is a company that owns and operates properties that produce income. This worked out quite well for Mamiko for two reasons. She would become a landowner (if only by proxy), and it would provide her with some return on her investment.

The properties these REITs own are shopping centers, apartment buildings, offices, hotels, warehouses, and other spaces used commercially. REITs are essentially the "landlord." These companies also can be involved in the financing of these properties.

REITs have shares that are traded publicly on the stock exchange. However, the similarities to stocks end there. When a REIT qualifies, it can operate free of corporate tax. What a REIT does is quite simple and elegant at the same time. These companies give back to their shareholders at least 90 percent of the company's taxable income. In some cases, 100 percent is paid back to shareholders. These dividends, which are essentially the operating profits divided among the owners, are then deducted from their tax bill.

This was a custom-fit for Mamiko. In her halting English she had told me that no one in her family had ever owned anything. She then proceeded to tell me what she had learned.

"American Congress created REIT." She told me that they did this "so we can buy big things on small budget." She was right on that account. In 1960, Congress did allow the investment in large-scale, income-producing properties to be made available to small-scale investors like you and Mamiko.

She said, "REIT companies have many rules. Best rule is sharing income and keeping losses." I mentioned that the company must share the income with the shareholders, but the losses cannot be passed on in the way the profits are.

These companies need to be involved in the business of real estate, such as owning and collecting rents, be taxable as a corporation, and have at least 100 shareholders. One thing Mamiko as a novice investor missed in her excitement is the provision that says that no more than 50 percent of the total outstanding shares can be held by five or fewer investors during the last half of each taxable year. This allows a greater number of shareholders a vote in the company's business.

REITs, despite their special tax treatment, are essentially publicly traded companies that invest in real estate as their main business. With 149 companies trading on the New York Stock Exchange, 12 on the NASDAQ, and 27 on the American Stock Exchange, finding the right one, as Mamiko discovered, can prove to be "very difficult."

While all REITs are involved in real estate, not all of them perform the same function. For instance, equity REITs develop and fund properties that they keep and maintain as income-producing parts of the company. Mortgage REITs are lenders to properties that need credit. These are not companies that provide private mortgages to individuals; instead, they lend to large customers who further develop their properties. And then there are companies that do both.

REITs can be further broken down into additional categories based on what they own and operate. Some specialize in commercial properties, others in apartments, and still others may operate hospitals or hotels. Mamiko also found out that she could find a local company that "uses my money where I can see it." REITs also can be geographic in nature, investing in certain areas.

In Chapter 7 we saw how investing in bonds was affected by inflation. Inflation, as you may recall, is the cost of a product in today's dollars as compared with previous dollars. Inflation, if it is kept in check, can raise the prices of goods, which can increase the amount of money a company can earn. This, in turn, increases jobs and starts a cycle that is good for the economy. However, that same inflation can harm the money you will get in the future. The value of a dollar now will be worth far less 20 years from now. A dollar in 1963 would need to grow to $5.98 in 40 years to have the same buying power.

Inflation has what can be called a "corrosive" effect on your returns. But this is not the case with REITs. In an environment where inflation or the cost of living rises, rents tend to follow. This increases dividends, which keep pace with inflation. This is a general principle, keep in mind, and a special circumstance that makes REITs attractive not only to individual investors but also to folks looking for a good tax-deferred investment in their IRA or 401(k).

I asked Mamiko if she understood the risks of owning a REIT. She explained it more or less this way: "All property has risk. Businesses that own property know this. If the economy is good, I make money. If the economy is bad, good businesses cover themselves." Good economies see strength in properties as businesses spend more on expansion, hoping to capture prosperity. New apartments are built. Factories, stores, and offices all become necessary parts of the good times. But economies don't always remain vibrant. Sluggish economies can see businesses scale back, workers laid off, and spending slow. This is definitely a negative.

REITs have come a long way. They understand that not all parts of the country feel the effects of the economy in the same way. What might be a downturn in Joliet may be a boom in El Paso. Companies tend to diversify themselves, a method that spreads the risk over a wide area.

There was once a time when this industry did a bad job at figuring the values of properties. This led to lending that created an enormous problem in the early nineties. The problem has been corrected, and REITs have become a conservative bright spot in the world of investing.

Only a portion of Mamiko's problem was solved. She still needed to know where to put her money. She told me that she understood what a dividend was and liked the idea of getting a piece of the profit back for her investment. She liked the idea that she was buying something real that would last a long time. She laughed when she said, "No straw houses on a beach with big waves for me."

It is important to understand the difference between a REIT and actually owning property. Mamiko never really wanted to become a direct owner.

She enjoyed the freedom of moving about, but she had a deep desire to satisfy her grandfather's wishes and buy property. REITs are not the same as houses in terms of investments. Over the last 25 years or so, the average price of a house, as published by the Federal Home Loan Mortgage Corporation, has increased a little over 5½ percent. This figure is based on a compounded annual interest rate. Some of you know exactly what I am talking about. Others have seen the value of their home skyrocket. On average, though, your home, while important to you, is not an investment. It does not produce income. Refinancing your home and getting a big equity check is not income; it is a bigger loan—a loan that needs interest paid on it. The property also requires upkeep. Commercial real estate, however, is a whole different situation.

There are several ways to add REITs to your investments, but you need to do a certain amount of research. The National Association of Real Estate Investment Trusts has a great Web site (*http://nareit.com*) that can show you the performance of its members, in many instances actually comparing them with other trusts in the same category. Supplied with the ticker symbol and some well-done investigation, all you need is a broker to make the transaction. There is no minimum required to invest, although the brokerage house is going charge a commission.

(If you would like to do it yourself, at the end of this chapter I provide a partial list of companies who sell REITs as part of a mutual fund. I do suggest, however, that you do two things: Always read the prospectus that comes with the fund, and second, read Chapter 9 thoroughly. In it you will find many of the terms we sort of brushed over—terms such as *risk* and *diversification*—as well as an explanation of what a mutual fund is and how mutual funds can make your money and protect it.)

Mamiko began making her investments in this area using REIT mutual funds, first using an index fund and then branching out into industry-specific funds. Like bond funds, REIT funds invest in a wide variety of companies that just happen to be REITs. As with all mutual funds, the risk is spread among many companies.

SAFE AS A COOKIE JAR

One short step up from stashing money under the mattress and an un-FDIC-insured brother of a savings account, money market funds provide conservatism by the bucket load. They were created in 1972 as a way of offering higher yields to investors who wanted a good return without much in the way of real risk. Twenty years ago these funds were yielding a healthy 5.5 percent. Now many elderly investors who sought these safe havens are getting not much more than a 1 percent return on their investment. And that is before inflation is calculated into the equation. If you begin using even the low inflation rates, these funds are earning almost nothing.

Money market accounts are mutual funds (which we will explore in greater depth in Chapter 9) that invest, as a group, in high-yielding debt. Money markets are based on the value of a dollar. This is a constant price that allows investors who want to move into cash to have a clear-cut position. If you buy $1000 worth of a money market fund, it will be worth $1000. This constant balance, coupled with the opportunity to earn some serious interest, caused the growth of this category to explode. You can now pick from over 1300 funds.

Money market mutual funds also offered the investor liquidity. *Liquidity* is a fancy word for "cash on demand." Working just like a checking account in most instances, money market funds allow investors to withdraw money from their accounts with a simple check. Access and liquidity made these accounts perfect for older investors. Add in some interest for your business, and these accounts became very popular. While these privileges vary from institution to institution, they are essentially the same.

After that, the decision is whether to go tax-free or taxable. These two types of funds vary only in how they invest. Tax-free funds tend to buy tax-free municipal bonds and other obligations whose returns are not taxed at the state or federal level. Taxable funds invest in short-term government debt.

In difficult investing environments, investors use these accounts as a safe haven. Acting like a passive security system, the Security and Exchange Commission (SEC) has made sure that these funds are as safe as possible. The SEC has demanded better diversification as an additional measure to protect against "bad paper," or debt that companies can't pay, a principle in investing ignored by far too many people even now.

Many elderly people have felt the pinch of these low interest rates largely because they no longer earn any money outside of Social Security. The most common type of fund these people put their money into for safe keeping is called a *direct-obligations-only money fund.*

These funds, while not insured by the FDIC, are invested in the next best thing, the debt of the federal government. The investors who use these types of funds have put their money to work in funds that invest only in U.S. Treasury securities.

Expenses, which I will get into in more detail a little later on, can come from many sources. The manager needs to be paid. The banks that hold the investor's money charge custodial fees. There are legal fees, advisory fees, distribution fees, and sometimes 12-pound fees, all of which eat into the slim chance that the money will earn any income at all. While low-interest-rate environments are not the norm, the near-zero return makes these investments as a safe as a cookie jar.

I have listed some funds below that by no means are recommendations. The following funds are invested in Treasury bills as their entire portfolio:

Vanguard MMR/U.S. Treasury Portfolio (800/662-7447)

Dreyfus 100% U.S. Treasury MMF (800/782-6620)

T Rowe Price U.S. Treasury Money Fund (800/638-5660)

The following funds invest in direct-obligation-only securities issued by the U.S. government:

Fidelity U.S. Government Reserves (800/544-8888)

Dreyfus BASIC Government Money Market Fund (800/782-6620)

Real Estate Mutual Funds

As promised, here is the list of mutual funds that specialize in REITs. Be aware of three things when you begin your search: First, you want your fund to be low in expenses and, if possible, initial deposits. This is most often the case in an index fund (see Chapter 9). Second, you want the fund to be a no-load fund. This type of fund does not charge a fee when you invest (front-end load) or when you withdraw (closed-end load) your money. These fees put a drag on your return. And third, always have a good understanding about risk. Nothing is without risk, save stuffing cash in a jar. With the right understanding of this concept, however, you can make a choice that provides you with enough comfort to see your investment through.

ABN-AMRO Real Estate Fund (800/443-4725)

Advantus Real Estate Securities Fund (800/665-6065)

AIM Real Estate Fund (800/959-4246)

Alliance Real Estate Investment (800/227-4618)

Alpine International Real Estate Equity Fund, Alpine U.S. Real Estate Equity Fund, Alpine Realty Income and Growth Fund (888/785-5578)

American Century Real Estate Investments (800/345-3533)

Aon REIT Index Fund (800/266-3637)

Brazos/JMIC Real Estate Securities (800/426-9157)

CDC Nvest AEW Real Estate Fund (800/862-4863)

CGM Realty Fund (800/345-4048)

Cohen & Steers Equity Income Fund, Cohen & Steers Realty Shares, Cohen & Steers Special Equity Fund (800/437-9912)

Columbia Real Estate Securities (800/547-1707)

CRA Realty Shares (800/932-7781)

Davis Real Estate Funds (800/279-0279)

Delaware REIT Fund (800/523-1918)

Deutsche Real Estate Securities (800/730-1313)

DFA Real Estate Securities (310/395-8005)

Eii Realty Securities Fund (888/323-8912)

Excelsior Real Estate Funds (800/446-1012)

FBR Realty Fund (888/888-0025)

Fidelity Real Estate Investment (800/544-8888)

First American Real Estate Investment Funds (800/637-2548)

Firstar Select REIT Fund (800/677-3863)

Flag Investors Real Estate Securities Fund (800/767-3524)

Forward Uniplan Real Estate Investment Fund (800/999-6809)

Franklin Real Securities Estate Fund (800/342-5236)

Frank Russell Real Estate Securities (800/787-7354)

Fremont Real Estate Securities Fund (800/548-4539)

Gabelli Westwood Realty Fund (800/937-8966)

GMO REIT Fund (617/346-7641)

Goldman Real Estate Funds (800/621-2550)

Hancock Real Estate Funds (800/225-5291)

Inland Real Estate Income and Growth Fund (800/828-8999)

INVESCO Advisor Real Estate Fund (800/525-8085)

Johnson Realty (800/541-0170)

Kensington Strategic Realty Fund, Kensington Select Income Fund (800/253-2949)

LaSalle U.S. Real Estate Fund (800/527-2553)

Lend Lease U.S. Real Estate Securities Fund, Lend Lease European Real Estate Securities Fund (877/563-5327)

Mercantile Diversified Real Estate Fund (800/551-2145)

Merrill Lynch Real Estate Funds (800/995-6526)

Morgan Stanley Dean Witter Real Estate Fund (800/548-7786)

Munder Real Estate Equity Investment Fund (800/438-5789)

Neuberger Berman Real Estate Fund (800/877-9700)

Phoenix Real Estate Securities Funds (800/243-4361)

Pioneer Real Estate Funds (800/225-6292)

Principal Real Estate Funds (800/247-4123)

ProFunds Ultra Real Estate Funds (888/776-3637)

Prudential Real Estate Securities Fund (800/225-1852)

RREEF Real Estate Securities (888/897-8480)

Security Capital Real Estate Funds (888/732-8748)

Spirit of America Investment Fund (800/367-3000)

SSGA Real Estate Fund (800/647-7327)

Stratton Monthly Dividend REIT Shares (800/634-5726)

T. Rowe Price Real Estate Fund (800/638-5660)

Third Avenue Real Estate Value Fund (800/443-1021)

UAM Heitman Real Estate Funds (877/826-5465)

Undiscovered Managers Fund (888/242-3514)

The Vanguard REIT Index Portfolio (800/662-7447)

Van Kampen U.S. Real Estate Fund (800/421-5666)

Victory Real Estate Investment Fund (800/539-3863)

Wells S & P REIT Fund (800/282-1581)

DRAWING CONCLUSIONS

REITs, like all investments, can suffer losses. But many of these have become quite nimble and profitable in the process. Because of the tax situation involved with the distribution of the profits, a REIT is best placed in a tax-deferred account such as a traditional IRA or a 401(k) plan.

- Money market accounts usually are present in every 401(k) situation. Be aware that any money that has not been directed by you to a specific investment will be placed in these low-interest accounts. Don't let this happen. Money markets do not hold any significant place in a long-range retirement plan. Use them as a temporary holding place for large sums of money, such as an insurance payout or the proceeds from a home sale.

- Mamiko lives on the fringes of our economy but is unwilling to be ignored. Investors should be active in their financial well-being, even if that means getting politically active as well. Warren Buffet once suggested that an investment, properly researched, should be able to hold its own for a year without doing anything. He is right about this for two reasons. People generally are nervous Nellies when it comes to investing, even if they have a long-range horizon. They like to tend to and tinker with their decisions.

- The other reason this well-renowned investor is right is that long range is longer than most people realize, and the effects of leaving an investment alone in most cases will allow that investment to weather through several cycles. The best advice is to check your statements when they come in, pay attention to any changes in your manager's investment style, and otherwise relax.

9

Step 9: Don't Buy Stocks

We have landed on Mars, and Jacob and I couldn't be more excited. Space fans are usually not as easy to find as he was. We actually work in the same building.

We have been following the program from the launch of the Spirit exploration program to the touchdown on January 3, 2004. While the pictures it has sent back look as if the Martian landscape holds little promise, Jacob and I know that it does.

It takes exactly this kind of enthusiasm, this spirit of adventure, and this commitment to the mission to develop a successful retirement plan as well. Much like the jubilant scientist at NASA's Jet Propulsion Laboratory who jumped for joy as the first 10 feet of the lander rolled from its pod, we also should relish the small successes in our plans as we gather momentum. *Momentum* is a science word meaning "force, drive, or energy," which is all you ever want from a good plan.

I love science. It has penetrated my writings for quite some time, mostly in an effort to educate the financial reading public that there is more to life than dollar signs. I've used Max Plank's theory of quantum mechanics, I've drawn similarities to the string theory (another guess on how the universe is connected), and I've even tried to develop a theory of everything designed just for money. But space is always the best metaphor for your financial life.

Jacob, as I mentioned much earlier in this book, is a mutual fund collector. To me, it's no real surprise, nor is it odd that he is also looking to the heavens the same way he looks at his investments—with wonderment and hope. He knows that any plan that relies on decisions made today will not be perfect by any means. No one knows how this whole thing we call life will turn out. Will looking into space reveal something we are better off not knowing, or will it provide the answers to the many questions we have brought to the journey? Does using mutual funds as a part of your retirement planning hold much of the same unknown answers to our questions? Science and the science of investing both hold the same kinds of possibilities. Remember the old theme song for "Lost in Space" that suggested that "it was about time, it was about space. . . ."

So how do we decide the right place, the right time, and the right method? It is easier than you might imagine. Just like traveling to a distant place, your trip will only hold special meaning if you learn something about your destination. These journeys are, as the saying goes, what you bring to them. That "something" is the information contained in this next step of your investing life. This is the right place at the right time. I believe that I also have the right method.

Before we go too much further, though, there are some basic terms that need a little clarification. There are words used in everyday financial conversation that might lack real meaning for the average person. Assuming that you bring a basic knowledge to investing, far too many people who talk about money or write about it make the basic assumption that you know some of the basic terms. As we go along in this chapter, I promise not to make that assumption. First, however, we need a brief introduction to some of the players in this wide world of money.

Over the years, I have found that the biggest confusion comes in separating the economy from the markets. Politicians are especially guilty of intertwining these two things as if they were somehow the same beast. In fact, one is real, and the other is only a figment of your imagination. Or depending on whom you are listening to, vice versa.

The economy is an abstract idea whose ability to be downright difficult and unpredictable is evident time and again. Presidents and their congresses have attempted to fix the economy, help it or otherwise, and bend it to their will, all in the hope that it will aid them in their attempt at reelection. A strong economy is always something a politician would like to take credit for having repaired or enabled—or even better, created. Elected officials, in their misguided and overly lobbied way, will raise taxes and cut taxes.

They run surpluses (rarely—a *surplus* is more than is needed) and deficits (mostly—a *deficit* is less than is needed) all in an attempt to tweak the economy to shine a favorable light on their term in office. Their success or failure with this manipulation is often not their fault. They can't help themselves. But the real blame falls to the economist who may have had their ear. So the government has a hand in the economic outcome of your plan.

The Federal Reserve (the Fed), the central bank, creates monetary policy. Its actions of lowering or raising interest rates allow the economy enough room to grow or, in some cases, retreat from over-exuberance. This board of big bank governors, learned economists each and every one of them, looks at facts and figures available to the public and some information not generally known to determine the economy's overall well-being. This group cuts the interest rate (the rate charged to the biggest banks for an overnight loan) to help stimulate growth by providing money to borrow that is cheap. It raises the interest rate to slow the economy from an exhaustive run to a more manageable walk. Add to this the obsessive concern of the Fed about inflation, and the Fed has many people listening when it speaks. Whatever the Fed does, keep in mind that it takes months to work. The actions of the Fed will have an effect on the credit markets mostly. This means that Fed policies may change interest rates and yields over a wide area, including housing, bonds and other fixed-income securities, and money market funds.

The Treasury Department has the job of keeping the dollar strong and healthy. This makes our currency the money of choice when folks around the world want to do business. This also involves a complicated question of balance that is often very elusive. The work of this department can help or hurt trade with international customers of the companies who employ us. This department also accommodates the funding of the government. When the Treasury Department issues and auctions off Treasury notes, it is actually raising money for the government. The Treasury Department is in essence the nation's piggy bank.

Business, a player from the private sector, simply does what it has done successfully for thousands of years. It produces products or services and, in turn, sells those products or services to us for a profit. Every idea, every notion follows this simple pattern. To invent a widget, you need an idea. You raise money (investors) to make your widget, buying raw materials (the first line of purchase), create your product, and begin to sell it so that you can create more widgets. Perhaps you find a better way to produce them, and you pass the cost of this innovation on to the folks who spend—us.

We are consumers. If you listen closely, you find out that consumers keep the whole game afoot. We are the 800-pound gorillas. We sit where we want, when we want. We do the same thing with our money. We spend where we want, when we want. And in doing so, we give all the players their reason for being.

We spend because businesses create things that we need. By doing that, our dollars allow businesses to produce more widgets. The spending we provide contributes an enormous amount of the economic bottom line. In fact, two-thirds of the purchasing in this country is done by us. It is no wonder that economists are concerned about us.

You often hear about different organizations conducting surveys and studies that watch for changes in our attitudes or, as it is sometimes called, our sentiments. Or perhaps they survey us for our "confidence" in how we feel about the economy. They track our buying habits. They study our moods. They want to know how we think so that they in turn can react. All this information is then taken, compiled, studied, and analyzed, and some basic decisions are made about how we will spend. Because we spend, the whole economic world spins. We are the economy. Remember that.

The people who do all this observing and do it best are the economists, the "dismal scientists." It seems that one day a man named Malthu made a gloomy prediction that population would always grow faster than food, and that, he suggested, spelled doom for humankind. We were destined for "unending poverty and hardship." This "dismal" outlook was how the term for economists was born.

Economists study the economy. They poke at it, prod it, and try to understand why it does what it does. Economists create scientific models of what we do, how we react in certain situations, and why. This information is apparently essential for businesses to run more efficiently. Why produce widgets, the thinking goes, if the marketplace really wants a locomotive? But opinions can vary widely in this group. What some hold as empirical truths are often up to be challenged by some new free thinker. There is an old saying that goes something like this: "You can lay all the economists in the world end to end and still not reach a conclusion."

Economists study markets. Markets simply react to supply and demand. Economists attempt to measure the demand so that markets can provide supply.

Now we can throw the poor investor into the mix. With the game already in full swing, you try to find your place on the board. Most of us do so with varying degrees of success.

It is time to harness all those pieces of information and tie them together. There are two types of investors: those who understand risk, and those who do not. Investors all start with the same goal. How they eventually arrive at that goal, however, is the real story.

Risk is an interesting thing. Much different from the risk that might be involved in an extreme sport, investment risk plays on a much higher level. Rather than seeing the challenge that lies before you, investment risk presents the need for an ability to look inward at yourself while looking outward at the same time. This is not even the worst of it.

We have discussed throughout this book the need for a plan, the understanding that your plan will take time to unfold, and that you will try to enjoy yourself getting there. Risk, like some sort of twisted puzzle, not only can help you get there but also can derail your plans just as easily.

Thus the very first thing is to ask someone—preferably your financial partner, that person you have chosen as your monetary sounding board and that someone who is willing to offer his or her honest opinion when asked about yourself—"Am I a gambler?"

Don't get me wrong; risk is not gambling, but gambling involves risk and sometimes can provide a good measuring stick for how you approach your investments. Personally, I am a horrible gambler. Stories abound among those close to me about my inability to pick a winner. So does that make me a horrible investor as well? No, it doesn't.

Risk is not gambling. Risk is, instead, an understanding of the value of the money that you have earned, the time in front of you or your investing horizon, and your ability to let the investment work.

Risk is also opportunity. The person who puts his or her money under the mattress still has the money because he or she has taken absolutely no risk. Inflation will erode the value of that money, making it worth less, but the person will still have it, intact and available.

Once you understand that to make your money grow, you will need to invest it, you will have taken an important step. The right amount of risk will get you there.

I have taken a decidedly bottoms-up approach in this book for good reason. Risk is like stepping into a cold pool of water. It is bracing at first, but gradually, you become accustomed to it. Understanding that investments are very similar, somewhat frightening at the beginning until we become familiar with the environment, can make the experience much more pleasurable and rewarding.

To summarize, risk is needed to beat inflation and to make your money grow. It should be used carefully and thoughtfully. And finally, it should not add any stress to your life. Your investments are part of a plan to gradually wind down your working life. Getting there shouldn't be all about amassing a great fortune. It should be about enjoying life on the way. Now the only thing to do is to find the right amount of risk to make your plan work for you.

When I first meet Talia, she was suffering from a disease called *myopic loss aversion*. While not painful or even really a disease, this condition still gave Talia unnecessary discomfort.

She had built up a sizable portfolio of mutual funds in her 401(k) plan at work, spreading her investments over 10 different funds. Thanks to the Internet, she was able to monitor the minute movements of her funds on a daily basis. And this was the source of her problem. Friend and frequent contributor to my Web site, Larry Swedroe, called this the "equity risk premium puzzle." The puzzle, he once wrote, is the fear of short-term losses, a preoccupying thought even though there have been very few periods in the history of the stock market where it has been down. Panic sets in at the slightest change in how people think their investments are performing. Being goal-oriented is good, but overthinking the end result can be destructive.

Dollar-cost averaging (DCA) helped Talia with this problem. She had pumped enormous amounts of money, all pre-tax, into her retirement plan at work. As long as her mutual funds were going up, she felt as though her plan was working just fine. When it was evident that the value of those same mutual funds was beginning to slide, she stopped contributing altogether. This creates a missed opportunity that makes true long-term investors cringe.

DCA is a passive style. It keeps your money involved in good times and bad. The concept holds that by investing a steady stream of money, you'll find that the market has more bottoms than tops. Those bottoms are your bread and butter, so to speak. The principle is simple: If you buy a share of a mutual fund for a dollar, it is worth a dollar. If the market goes up 50 percent, you get a smaller share for your dollar. So a share is worth half of what it was when you initially invested. Instead of one dollar buying you one share, you now have 0.5 of a share. But suppose that the reverse were to happen and the fund's share value dropped by 50 percent. That same dollar now has you in possession of 1.5 shares, buying you an additional half share.

The problem is that we have a difficult time purchasing something for less when it comes to equity mutual funds. Clothes, cars, and durable goods are considered bargains when they sell for less than what we would consider fair value. But our investments take on a much different criterion. DCA helps you to bring some discipline to your investing.

Over the last 6 decades, the stock market has performed better in the months between October and April than during the other 6 months of the year. With few exceptions, the Standard & Poor's 500 Index, a popular index that follows the top 500 publicly traded companies, has seen the value of its collective shares drop in the summer months only to regain their value in the fall and winter months.

In 1982, for example, equities bought from this index in those spring and summer months would have shown only a gain of 3.5 percent. By the end of the winter, those same stocks would have returned 36.5 percent. DCA would have allowed you to purchase many more shares at a lesser value over the summer months, leading to higher year-end worth of your investments. More recently, the same scenario played out in 1998 (summer, –9 percent; winter, up 31 percent), 1999 (summer, –4 percent; winter, up 13 percent), 2001 (summer, –17 percent; winter, up 4 percent), and 2002 (summer, –24 percent; winter, up 13 percent). Human behavior has the majority of us looking at the summer months as the most risky. The markets are down, and who wants to "throw good money after bad"? DCA takes that part of the problem out of the equation. The temptation to buy equities when the market is on the way up and is near its top is greater than the reverse. Before we move on, the result of those 6 decades has the summer months returning less than 1 percent and the winter months with gains of more than 9 percent. The returns for a DCA investor would have been much higher.

Talia, whose investment horizon is based on the possibility that she will work until she is in her sixties, realizes now that she has 30 more years to buy at market lows, a more frequent event than market highs, building up an increased number of shares in those down times.

One of the finest examples of how DCA works involves a coin and two heads of state. President Jackson once gave a gift to the Sultan of Muscat. It was an 1804 silver coin and was nicknamed the "Sultan." A family of rich folks from Vermont bought the "Sultan" in 1945 for $5000. The coin was then placed in a vault somewhere where it didn't see the light of day for the next 54 years—until, of course, it was auctioned off for $4.14 million!

Wow, you might just say to yourself. Why should I invest in mutual funds when I could be buying rare and old coins? I'll tell you why you shouldn't. If those collectors had taken the same cash and invested it in a mutual fund indexing (copying) the Standard & Poor's 500, with the dividends reinvested, they would have made about $400,000 more. And that would be without factoring in the cost of the auctioneer and the 15 percent buyer's fee.

Now, you may not have to plunk five grand down and wait 54 years for the payoff. Plunk $100 down, and do it consistently for months and even years, and you will have benefited from similar compounding results.

DCA allows compounding to work its magic on your investments, creating wealth over time. In the meantime, though, take a moment to examine that change jar on your dresser.

MaeLyn, a young businesswoman with a flower shop in suburban Baltimore, found herself spending three sick, flu-addled days in bed back in 1999. Unable to do much more than watch television, she huddled close to a box of tissues and an assortment of fluids and rediscovered how little interest she had in daytime television—until she found CNBC. CNBC, for the uninitiated, is the business arm of NBC's cable division. Along with the upwardly mobile markets of the late nineties, this station, tickers crawling across the bottom of the screen, had become the television of choice of this "new" investor age. It was on sets everywhere, a marathon of financial information—until the bottom fell out.

Until that moment, MaeLyn had been concentrating on building her business, a task that demanded all her attention. But that day in March, she watched the Dow Jones Industrial Average, a group of 30 stocks picked by the *Wall Street Journal,* surge pass the 10,000 mark. She had only been vaguely aware of this historic moment and was even more transfixed by the celebration that ensued.

The folks on the screen seemed caught up in the euphoria, all the while cautioning that this was only a number. MaeLyn was impressed by the celebration. She had been so wrapped up in her own goals that she had missed the meteoric rise of the index to that level. She felt as though she was missing something. So she called her father at his office in Baltimore.

Her father greeted her warmly and expressed concern at her germ-riddled voice. But he took the time to explain what all the hoopla was about. "Take my advice, Mae. Pay no attention to those stock jockeys talking up all those companies. Don't buy stocks," he said, suggesting instead that she buy mutual funds.

Her father explained that mutual funds were a pool of investors who shared the same goals. People who invest in mutual funds know that the markets are a treacherous and even dangerous place for individuals, and because of that, they have enlisted a professional to direct their investments for them. Mutual fund managers, he explained, were different from stock-brokers. Brokers were merely the conduits for the investor, he explained. They did what you told them to do. They offered advice and in-house research, and they were supposed to help you grow your money. And, he added, he supposed that they did. However, he was not comfortable with the cost of that type of partnership.

Mutual funds, he explained, were different. MaeLyn was taking notes as he spoke. When he got going on a subject, you always took notes. Funds generally are made up of an advisory team, her father continued. They are governed by a board of directors that makes sure they follow a charter, or a set of investment rules. Each mutual fund has some sort of strategy. It might be growth or value, balance or aggressiveness. The board keeps an eye on the manager of the fund, making sure he doesn't stray from the plan.

This was a way of spreading the risk of picking the wrong stocks. He was not so sure that it was a perfect method, but it was a much better one than going it alone. He did caution that there were certain rules that needed to be followed, and one thing that should always be kept in the back of her mind: Nothing financial is an easy ride. This concept, she told me later, had helped her and her two partners from college to survive the bumps in the road as they started their fledgling business.

Mutual funds disclose important investor information in a document called the *prospectus*. This is where the plan is contained, or the strategy that the fund uses to grow your money. This is the investment manual that is sent out by the mutual fund company telling you what it does, how it does it, and what you should know about how and what it does.

The first thing that you see is the "Key Information." Under the "Fund's Goals," usually written in one simple line, such as, "This fund seeks capital growth" (meaning that it is interested in taking a risk or two to make your money grow) or "This fund seeks capital appreciation" (meaning that the fund attempts to grow your money but at a more conservative, less risky pace), the fund tries to disclose its plan on how it will make your investment grow. While there are thousands of funds available, MaeLyn's father told her that the right choice is not as daunting as it might seem.

MaeLyn's father explained that the prospectus is required to outline the risk involved. He did warn her that this can come in somewhat muted language but that it should be plain enough to understand.

Looking for certain key words can be helpful. For instance, whenever you read the words, *actively traded,* he told her, it is a safe bet that you will be assuming some risk. Actively traded mutual funds have managers that pick from the companies their fund is chartered to use to reach your investment goals. This is why the key information is important. Understanding the fund's goals and trying to match them to yours is important.

Another type of investing takes on a more passive approach to growing your money. Index funds mimic a group of similar stocks of certain indexes such as the Standard & Poor's 500 Index, a grouping of the 500 largest companies, or the Russell 2000 Index, a collection of much smaller companies, for example.

The boundaries in an index fund, which is what the charter sets in place for the manager, are different from those of an active fund manager. An index fund will buy all the stock within those indices according to weight. A big company in an index may be carrying something the industry calls *weighting*. In other words, for the index to perform correctly, the largest companies need to be represented based on their contribution to the index's total return. This balancing act within the index is done by those who publish the list, and the fund manager needs only to match them to carry the index accurately.

Next, MaeLyn's father told her to look in the prospectus for the fund's performance. The only caution he offered was to be wary of the way these funds shed the most favorable light on themselves. Claiming they beat this index or that may not be the best way to measure how well a fund has done. Actively traded mutual funds should compare themselves with similar funds doing similar things. That may not make them look as good, though. Indexes are built a certain way to reflect a certain group. While this should be considered deceptive, it is still largely up to the investor to try to find out how a fund performed compared with its peer group or funds that invest in the same style or manner.

When MaeLyn's father sought to better explain it, he used a pool as an analogy. Divers cannot be compared with swimmers, even though they use the same body of water for their sport. It is the same with mutual funds. They all play in the same pool, but they each specialize in certain skills. He told her to try to find a fund that has finished in the top 10 percent over the last 3 years, not the last 12 months or even the last quarter. When a manager has been around for at least that amount of time, he has developed not only a pattern of trading but also a reliable gauge on how those choices have done. A good benchmark for performance is whether the fund has placed in the top 25 percent compared with similar funds over 3 years. He told MaeLyn that while looking for the top fund is tempting, what she really needs is to understand some other elements of the puzzle first.

Just remember, MaeLyn's father told her, you are buying into an investment philosophy. The higher the risk, the greater is the chance of rewards. The same is true for the flip side of the coin: The greater the risk, the greater is the chance for losses. Month-to-month fluctuations are not the issue here. Year-to-date returns are not the issue here. Investment style is the issue. More important is a consistent investment style over the long term.

Historical returns, 3 to 5 years, are a good benchmark. You should be looking at the tenure of the manager. In an actively traded mutual fund, it is all about the manager or the management team. Their abilities are what are being called into question.

Has the fund retained the services of the same manager over those years? Although funds will always point out that past results don't guarantee future returns, the fund manager's job is to return to you more money than you put in. If a fund has been successful in executing its plan, it probably will be able to continue to stick with it, making you money.

Expenses are next up on the list. MaeLyn's father was very emphatic about the next point, repeating himself to be sure that she understood. Always, always, always buy no-load funds. He told her that she should not have to pay any more than was absolutely necessary to make her money work, at least not up front.

Funds come in three basic types, he explained. A *front-load fund* takes a percentage of your investment skimmed off the top right up front, before you have even made a dime. Invest $1000 in a front-load fund charging you 5 percent, and you will have $950 put to work for you. Choose a *back-end-* or *closed-end-loaded fund,* he told her, a tone of distaste entering his voice, and a percentage will be taken after you chose to leave the fund, on money that the fund has made for you. You will always have to pay fees in a mutual fund, he told her, for the managers, the advisors, the custodians, and such, but you shouldn't have to pay fees *and* loads.

MaeLyn's father explained expenses this way: Keep them as low as possible. Each tenth, even hundredth of a percentage point eats away at your money. And these fees aren't waived if the fund loses money. Thus, if management is charging a rate that seems too high, chances are that you can find a similar fund with a similar objective doing it for less. He suggested that she use 1.5 percent as the high mark for her search. Keeping expenses at that level or lower would get her skilled management for cheap money.

Index funds are by far the least expensive. The reason, he told her, is because no one really needs to pay much attention to the stocks in the portfolio. The index has taken care of which stocks the fund owns and how much. Some funds are run by computer, some by management teams, and others by other funds. Their expenses can vary widely.

He told her that performance was the last issue on the list but that he would talk to her about that later. She was exhausted, her illness having taken a toll on her energy. He wished her better health and hung up.

When MaeLyn's mother caught wind of her illness, a different kind of risk she took by calling her father, she knew that a care package would arrive soon. Delivered by her younger brother the next day, the package had a wide assortment of motherly remedies for her cold and a box of information about mutual funds shipped by her father. In it she found a lengthy handwritten note further explaining her investment future. Her father, a small studio watchmaker, had shunned the world of personal computing, preferring to write his thoughts on paper. The letter was, she told us, written as if he had been waiting for this moment to share what he knew. She said that he probably just needed me to ask. She let me read the note, carefully worded and beautifully penned, each word seemingly drawn.

Dear Mae,

I enjoyed our conversation the other day. I hope that you are feeling better. Your mother is convinced that you will be on the road to recovery with the contents of this package. I just thought I'd pass on some additional thoughts on the subject of mutual funds while I am thinking about it. I apologize for not having talked to you about this before you moved out of the house. The opportunity never presented itself.

My biggest fear was that I left some things out of my explanation, or worse, you were in such a funk that you didn't remember what I had said.

Mutual funds are much more complicated than the prospectus tells you. I have included some prospectuses in the package for you to read. Before you do, though, let me explain some of the oddities of investing like this.

The first is the net asset value. You will see it referred to as NAV, and it is required by law to be tallied at the end of each business or market day. It is one way of determining the worth of a fund, but only if all the distributions, dividends, and interest payments are reinvested. Just keep reading, I'll explain.

Sometimes mutual funds sell stock they own at a profit. That profit is put back into the coffers in the form of cash called a *distribution*. This can affect the NAV, lowering it. This makes mutual fund price watching on a daily basis sort of silly. This distribution is almost always reinvested for you, unless, of course, you need the income. Which you don't. Some folks actually buy these things outside of retirement plans. Inside a retirement plan, though, you want to use the money to buy even more shares of the fund.

Dividends are paid by companies, not all of them, but the ones that do, do so from their profits. Dividends are a portion of the profit. The shareholders of a company believe that the profits are better used in the hands of the people who own the company, people like me and you, than left in the hands of the people who run the company. Good, often well-established companies pay dividends, and mutual funds that hold companies like these need to account for these payments. These are also, customarily, reinvested, buying you more shares of the fund.

Some of these funds, especially the ones that I own, tend to have a larger percentage of bonds in them. These also produce income in the form of interest payments. Add the two, the dividends and the interest payments, and you have what the fund calls *yield*.

Funds can have a zero yield and still can have a positive return. Aggressive funds that do not contain dividend-paying companies (aggressive growth firms seldom do, using the money instead to grow the company) or own any bonds tend to fall into this category. I am older than you, so yield means more to me than it would to someone your age.

But even I need to be cautious. Income is taxed at a higher rate than capital gains. In a mutual fund inside of a tax-deferred retirement plan like I am hoping you open, this is not a problem. The idea is that you are putting off the payment of those taxes until you are in a lesser tax bracket in retirement. Outside a retirement account, these distributions can be a real headache. So yield is based on income produced by the fund's holdings.

If you weren't good with numbers, I wouldn't bother explaining this to you. It is important that you know, though. It is important that you always have some idea where you stand financially. Taking care of the books for your little business has taught you that, I am sure. But even if you were not good with numbers, investing requires that you pay attention.

So a fund has stocks in it from many different companies. The value of these companies can rise, and in doing so, the NAV goes up also. But then the fund manager decides to sell some of those winning stocks. If the fund made money on the investment, you will be entitled to your cut. That's the capital gains distribution. When it does make this distribution, the NAV drops. That is because you now have stocks and cash. Your investment is safe and is worth more. NAV tells you the worth of the holdings, not the worth and the cash.

Here's how you can figure how well a fund has performed. Subtract your beginning position from your ending position. If, for example, you purchased 10 shares with an NAV of $10 ($100), suppose that when the end of the quarter arrived those shares were worth $12. The difference would be $20 [$120 (the new value) less $100 (the original value)]. Divide that by your beginning position of $100, and the quick answer is 0.2. Take that number, multiply it by 100, and you have figured out your total return without capital gains. In this case, your return is 20 percent. The investment has a zero yield. But if your fund has made a capital gains distribution and you have reinvested it, then you need to add the value of those new shares to your ending position.

You shouldn't have to worry too much about figuring performance just yet. I'll help you when the time comes. I just wanted you to know. The decision is ultimately yours, Mae, and you need to make a well-informed one.

Mutual funds, like the companies they buy for their portfolios, generally stick to certain styles. With so many companies to choose from, managers of these funds either become or are specialists. Their research teams are looking for certain things. Funds are monitored and rated by a variety of companies, all trying to help you understand the investment. The rating companies, the Morningstars and the Lippers of the world, are somewhat the same, the only difference coming in how they categorize funds. Morningstar usually breaks its funds down into three categories—large, middle, and small capitalization. *Capitalization,* commonly abbreviated as *cap,* suggests the size of the company based on its worth. Worth can change, however, sometimes very quickly. It is calculated based on the share price multiplied by the outstanding shares. For example, if a company is trading on the New York Stock Exchange for $10 a share and the company has 1 million shares circulating in the public domain, the worth of that company is $10 million. Large-cap funds tend to invest in companies worth $10 billion or more; middle caps find corporations in between $1 billion and $10 billion; small caps are whatever is left. Don't be fooled by size, though. Big companies can quickly become middle-cap or, worse, small-cap companies in an awful hurry.

Both Morningstar and Lipper have broken funds down even further to help investors understand what is called *style*. For instance, Morningstar breaks the funds it watches down into large growth, large blend, and large value. Lipper breaks its funds into large growth, large core, and large value. This is essentially the same, with essentially the same funds being rated. While many companies provide these kinds of tools to help you determine style, it is up to you to match their style with your investment plan.

What you need to look for in a mutual fund is what the fund does. If it invests in aggressive growth, count on what is called *volatility*. This means that the fund manager is going to try to grow your money using risk. Sticking their own (and your) neck out, they will take a chance, a well-researched one, on smaller companies with newer products and ideas that are usually on the edge of something big. Good fund managers will be able to recognize this potential, seize it, and make it work for you. Aggressive funds are not for the faint of heart. The rewards, when they come in, can be incredible. The losses can be gut-wrenching. To keep nimble, the manager of these funds does not look for income or dividends. Capital gains can be a real tax problem, though, unless you have your fund in a retirement account.

Growth funds can be a better bet and a somewhat safer one than their aggressive brothers. These kinds of funds invest in good companies that are focused on growing their businesses. They also tend to be more established companies. These funds may be less volatile, but don't be fooled; these funds also have a downside. Granted, if the market turns on growth funds, it can be a harsh wakeup call indeed. While aggressive growth funds are best suited for younger investors with long investment horizons, growth funds are best for the distance.

Some funds combine growth with income, which simply means that they will buy a few stocks that pay dividends, maybe preferred stocks or other income-producing securities to diversify themselves and to protect your investment.

For some people, spreading the risk is the best way for them to sleep comfortably at night. A balanced fund is a conservative creation whose main objective is to protect your principal. Such funds do this by purchasing high-dividend-paying stocks or even bonds. Once again, this is more for my age group, the older investor who is protecting all those years of growth. Balanced funds should be held in some percentage in a good portfolio if only for the diversity they offer. Without a lot of risk exposure, these funds tend to move slowly in one direction or the other. You always should pay some mind to diversity.

Value funds are run by managers who look for companies that are—and there is no better way to phrase it—undervalued. Managers in this group chase stocks that the rest of the investment community has overlooked usually in areas where growth is hard to establish but where making a profit from established business is a major attraction. You should take note of the fact that according to Morningstar, the difference in average return between value funds and growth funds over a 10-year period is not all that great.

Two things can happen to you without you knowing if you aren't careful when investing in mutual funds. The first one concerns exposure. With so many funds available, often investors purchase funds that are similar to other funds they already own. This creates an added possibility that you could own many of the same stocks in one fund as in the other. This is bad for two reasons: It increases your exposure to possible downside risk if a stock or a group of stocks does poorly, and it defeats the need to diversify your holdings. Mixing your funds according to style creates a good chance that if one fund style runs into trouble, the other might not. Large-cap funds may be taking a beating, for instance, while your small-cap fund is doing well. Value might beat growth one year, and growth might beat value the next. Be aware of exposure and diversity.

Personally, I would suggest that you stay away from international funds. Sure, they have done well and probably will do well in the future. My problem is controlling exposure and diversity. I have a tough enough time watching my money here at home. The other reason is that many companies are now global, and even though they are based in the United States, they take advantage of overseas markets to produce and sell their goods as well. Investing abroad just seems like something a much bigger player would need to achieve full diversity. Not me. And, I am supposing, not you either. But if you do, use an index fund for the investment.

There are other kinds of funds, and you might just take a fancy to some of them. There are the socially responsible funds designed for the "tree hugger" that might reside in you. There are funds that are run by nuns, and quite successfully I might add, whose charter is based on ethics. Funds also can be broken down into sectors, such as technology or health, and are for the more seasoned investor. There are funds that invest in REITs (that's real estate investment trusts, a real good idea and worthy of about 20 percent of your portfolio), and there are funds that invest in bonds (another place for 20 percent of your money).

Those last two, I think, you should index. Indexing is a popular way of spreading your risk over a broad range of companies in a specific group. Indexing with REITs is a good way to go, allowing you to invest in a number of different types of companies that buy, sell, rent, or lease properties. In the bond fund area, indexing is also an excellent idea.

You definitely could index your way through the remaining 60 percent of your portfolio and end up doing quite well over the long term, but I'm not so sure that is a good idea for someone your age. If you were 30 or even 40, I would say sure, at least half the 60 percent left should be in some sort of growth index, not too broad, so you don't have overlap in ownership. I mentioned that earlier because it is easy to do if you don't pay attention. If you were 50 (I'd be 80!), we would know two things at that point, Mae. You would know that your gene pool is rather robust. And you would know by realizing that "too conservative" at 50 might cost you later. You don't want to outlive your money. That, my dear, is the goal you are shooting for—enough to get you to the end without becoming a burden on your kids—our so-far-nonexistent grandchildren—or, worse, a burden on society.

At your tender age, though, you should be going for the gusto. These are your real compounding years. If you worked for some company that gave you a 401(k) and had matching funds, I would be encouraging you to save as much as possible. Even if it didn't have matching funds, I would still be pushing you. For future reference, should you ever get a job at a company that has such a plan or become a teacher or public worker, I can tell you the exact percentage you should sock away. The formula is easy. Figure out exactly what you need to take home each week based on your gross. Then start deducting 401(k) contributions by the percentage.

Keep adjusting this number in increments of 5 until you are withdrawing the maximum amount possible without disrupting your financial needs. Take 5 percent of your pretax first. If that doesn't affect your net take-home pay, add another 5 percent pretax. You don't want to make yourself cash-poor, but at the same time you do want to pay yourself first.

We did this with your cousin Vince. Uncle Seth and I suggested that he do this. Sure enough, he was saving 8 percent of his pretax income. That was just the right percentage to send him into a lower bracket, keeping his take-home almost the same as if he hadn't taken any deduction. Granted, he was probably right on the edge of the tax bracket. What he found out was that he could save even more without cramping his lifestyle. Seth didn't want him spiraling into debt because he was saving too much. In any event, the kid is saving about 15 percent of his pretax income. Like I said, for future reference. You know your little company can start a retirement plan. You and the boys should look into it.

I also mentioned compounding. This is the major benefit you get from investing. If you put away $100 and the interest paid on that money is 10 percent (using round numbers, but wouldn't that kind of return be nice?), you would have $110. The next time interest is calculated, it is done like this: 110×10 percent = 121. Given enough time, compounding in conjunction with dollar-cost averaging can seriously grow your money.

I think I mentioned on the phone the other day the importance of buying a no-load fund. Other than that, the only problem with investing in a mutual fund is your review of the manager(s). Some companies, I am told, have regular reviews of their employees. Do the same with your mutual fund manager. The manager does work for you, after all. Ask yourself if he is doing the job you hired him to do. Is he investing the way he said he would? Only by doing this periodically, such as once a year, will you know when to sell the fund. Research is easy. I can help you there. Buying is easy. I can offer some advice. But staying on board and selling are up to you.

A tried and true investor may know this, but someone as green as yourself should remember three things about investing. You may see lists of the top 10 reasons, or the 7 best methods, or 21 funds you need to own now, but pay no heed to them. Listen instead to your old man on this one, Mae.

Number 1: Ignore the economy and the markets. There will be politicians that will come in and ruin a perfectly good economy, and there will be ones who follow who fix it. It is the way things work. They raise taxes. They lower taxes. As for the markets, they will go up like so many Fourth of July explosions—pretty, impressive, but doomed to the history books. They will go down and sometimes stay down, victims of their own faltering exuberance. If you ignore both the economy and the markets, however, you will have no problem staying invested and become downright wealthy in the process.

Number 2: If you are taking advice from someone who is also in the business of selling a product, you must find another place for advice. I hope that some day you will be well-to-do. I prefer that to rich because having a daughter like you and being married to a woman like your mother have been a very wealthy experience for me. I am, because of who I am, doomed to be financially careful. I'll never have enough money to be flamboyant. But I will always have enough to be okay, if I am careful. It's a good life, but it requires patience and diligence. Manage your money wisely, and you won't need to pay for advice. I understand that financial planners need to make money to feed their families. Just don't let it be your money.

Number 3: Invest always. This sounds simple, but it is so important. It is a simple rule. Steady investing or paying yourself will have you thanking me when you are my age. If my father had emphasized that when I was younger, I would have been much better financially situated today. But I can't blame your Papa. He worked hard and made sure that each of his children was happy and healthy. His generation did not necessarily see the value of the stock market as part of a long-term plan. To his generation, it was using necessary cash on what seemed like a gamble. But you aren't getting off that easy. You will have the guilt of my words to haunt you, young lady, should you stray from this sensible and attainable objective.

That's all I have Mae. I hope this letter finds you in better health. I'm sure your mother's package will help.

Love,

Dad

This letter was the most useful advice a father could give an offspring. I was captivated by his concern for his daughter's financial future and, at the same time, making her responsible for it.

Long relegated to the category of boring, *index funds,* passive, usually inexpensive investments, have found their niche among investors. This was due largely to the ability of such funds to continue to produce numbers that not only are respectable but also in many cases and in terms of real returns have beaten actively managed funds.

When investors become concerned about their accumulated wealth, they tend to think in terms of lower risk. If they have built themselves a nice nest egg, protecting it in index funds allows them to keep their money in the market without too much exposure to risk. Indexed funds allow investors to keep their money involved in the market by spreading the risk among many stocks or bonds.

Indexed funds do offer some good protection to blue-class investors, but you should be warned: If the overall market is headed down, your fund will follow that market. The upside to something like that happening is that because of wide exposure and diversification to a variety of stocks, your index fund will have minimized losses.

In many indexed funds, the goal is not only to mimic the markets or provide diversification but also to be tax-efficient. I'll never forget when Jim Cramer, former hedge fund manager for TheStreet.com, shared rather loudly on television his distaste for what he described as "losing twice." Not only had an actively managed mutual fund that he had invested in lost money over the year, but he also was saddled with a tax bill.

Mr. Cramer should have understood, maybe even explained to his audience, why he had this problem. Selling stocks within an actively traded mutual fund usually incurs some sort of tax consequence. These types of funds often have some long-term holdings that have hefty gains in them. In other words, some of the stocks in companies were bought for much less than they are currently being priced. Selling those stocks creates a profit, and Uncle Sam wants his piece of the profit. The selling, for whatever reason, incurs a tax penalty. That tax liability, called *capital gains,* is passed on to you. It is the hidden expense that many fund owners ignore—until, that is, they find that much of their earnings are wiped out as a consequence. These types of surprises are especially painful when the value of your fund has declined also. That loss, however, doesn't prevent that tax bill from arriving. Those bills belong to the investor. It is the proverbial double whammy.

Index funds do not have this problem, with one exception. Periodically, indexes need to be rebalanced. Good companies are included, and companies that have lost their luster are eliminated. Then, and only then, do index funds change their holdings, and in the process, they sell the old holdings at a profit or a loss and buy the new companies. This will have a tax impact, but because it happens so infrequently, it is still very efficient taxwise.

Indexing has found renewed vigor among a wave of investors who have sought solace in this type of investing. Roughly two-thirds of all money invested finds its way into mutual funds. Looking toward indexing as a way to stay involved, investors have begun to understand some of the benefits of this type of investing.

Indexing isn't necessarily a no-brainer type of investment. When you are investing your money, even passive investments require some occasional monitoring. Index funds can charge a wide range of expenses for tracking a popular index such as the Standard & Poor's 500 Index. The Vanguard Group, founded and championed by John Bogle, the former chairman and the person most closely associated with the gospel of indexing, has some of the lowest expenses for its funds. Oddly, some fund families actually charge load fees for index funds. Imagine that! Avoid those funds altogether.

Funds that track the total market invest in all 6600 equities available across all exchanges. These *total-market funds* invest in a broad range of companies. Some index funds specialize or expand their specific index to cover additional stocks within a specified category. Domini Social Equity is one such fund that comes to mind. It tracks the Standard & Poor's 500 Index but adds another 150 or so companies to its list. Some of the more popular types of indexes are listed below:

Equity (Stock) Indexes

> Wilshire Large Growth (screens 750 largest U.S. stocks for sales growth and other growth indicators)
>
> Standard & Poor's 500 (500 of the largest U.S. stocks, both value and growth)

Wilshire Large Value (screens 750 largest U.S. stocks for lowest P/E and P/B ratios and highest yields)

Wilshire Mid-Cap Growth (screens 501st to 1250th largest U.S. stocks following the same criteria as Wilshire Large Growth)

Standard & Poor's 400 (501st to 900th largest U.S. stocks, both value and growth)

Wilshire Mid-Cap Value (screens 501st to 1250th largest U.S. stocks following same criteria as Wilshire Large Value)

Wilshire Small Growth (screens 751st to 2500th largest U.S. stocks following same criteria as Wilshire Large Growth)

Russell 2000 (1001st to 3000th largest U.S. stocks, both value and growth)

International Indexes

International Indexes MSCI The World (captures 60 percent of every developed country's market capitalization and industry sectors, including the United States)

MSCI EAFE (captures 60 percent of market cap and industry for 20 countries in Europe, Australia, and the Far East, excluding the United States)

MSCI Emerging Markets (applies MSCI criteria to countries identified as emerging by in-house guidelines)

Bond Indexes

Lehman Brothers Long-Term Govt/Corp (Treasury, agency, and corporate bonds with face values more than $100 million and maturities of at least 10 years)

Lehman Brothers Interm-Term Govt/Corp (same criteria as Lehman Brothers Long-Term, but maturities of at least 1 year and less than 10 years)

A final word about indexes is in order. They do not necessarily buy every stock in the index. Some companies are too small, and because of that, funds cannot purchase shares. If they did, these companies would have inflated share prices because there just isn't a lot of stock to buy. Stock prices, if you weren't already aware, are based on supply and demand. Smaller companies have less stock on the open market. Sudden interest in a small company's stock can send the price unnaturally upward. Because of their small size, this creates what is called a *liquidity problem*. This, in turn, creates problems with weighting and balancing. In other words, more mess than it is worth.

Index funds mimic the index they follow. A fund that mimics the Wilshire 5000 probably does not own all 5000 companies but rather a select portion of them. Once again, some companies are just too small.

When you buy shares in a mutual fund, you usually purchase them with all the high-hoped optimism of a child at the circus. You want performance. You want the golden ring. You want to be the one who makes his or her wealth as easily as possible.

In the real world of investing, as Jacob found out, things aren't always that easy. Funds falter, markets stumble, and things change. You change.

Fund managers leave. Perhaps the funds focus has changed. Sometimes funds become too large and close their doors to new investors. Sometimes funds simply lose their way, trying to find the right place to be, a chore that has become increasingly difficult over the last 3 to 4 years. Sometimes these events give you cause to wonder, "Should I sell?"

Although I don't suggest that you ever buy stocks individually, some of the same advice employed by them can be applied to a mutual fund investor. This sage wisdom demands that you do two things: Know when to sell, and follow your own plan.

Jacob had one thing going for him and one thing decidedly working against him. He understood that the investment horizon was much like the Martian landscape beamed back from the Rover mission. The landscape appears rocky and forbidding to the naked and untrained eye. But to someone who knows what he's looking for, the promise of discovery, the hope of revealing something spectacular, and the belief that what you are doing holds hope for the future are not unlike what a mutual fund investor should do. They should have broad horizons that are full of hope. Jacob possesses this by the bucket load.

Knowing when to sell a mutual fund is a wholly different matter. Selling individual stocks is as easy as naming a percentage or a price that is tolerable to you. If, for instance, an individual stock falls below a certain mark, usually 8 to 10 percent of what you paid, your plan might suggest that you sell. Investors in mutual funds generally base their selling decisions on performance. If you have determined that a profit of 25 percent is acceptable, you also should sell. You also should set some sort of downside sell point, also based on performance.

Mutual fund managers also need to make similar decisions within their portfolios. Folks like Jacob have entrusted these managers with their hard-earned cash and have done so for good reason. They know what kind of investor they are. More important, these investors want their fund managers to follow the plan, invest with discipline, and first and foremost, make money.

Jacob is a collector. An avid business reader, he has a real problem saying no to a mutual fund. He has read all the popular advice but still finds himself doing the opposite. He has bought funds at the top time and time again. Over the course of the last 15 years, he has collected 40 mutual funds. When a fund falters, as many at the top of this year's "best of the bunch" list often do, he simply opens another account, letting his losses ride.

So why does he have such great difficulty selling these orphaned funds tucked in the back of his portfolio? He, like many investors, has a more difficult time understanding when the time to sell has arrived.

There are three basic things you should do to monitor your funds, all with an eye toward their health: First and foremost is the ability of your fund to keep pace with its peer group. Within the equity markets, there will always be better performers than others. If the group as a whole does better, though, for even as little as one quarter, and your fund has failed to keep in step, you probably should take another hard look at your fund. A hard look is not a sell signal but a "watch list" of sorts.

Small caps will have their day, but not usually at the same time the big caps will. Value will shine when the markets turn bearish, but growth and all of its volatile brethren will do better once confidence in the market returns. This is the way the markets work. If your fund fails to do what the rest of the group has done, however, it might be time to think about selling.

Should this fund continue to underperform and the quarterly letter that fund manager sends you is not answering your question, perhaps its time to sell. Selling the fund does not mean cashing it in for money unless you are holding the fund outside your retirement plan. Rather, take the fund's assets and roll them over to another fund that has been following the criteria we talked about earlier.

Another excellent indicator of your fund's health is a market rally. These events tend to bring all stocks up as enthusiasm brings buyers back into the market. However, if your fund failed to find it's footing in this type of recovery, then you probably should begin to ask yourself why. Once again, if the answer is not to your liking, sell the fund.

Second, you don't often have access to all the insider news about whether a fund manager has lost her touch. You should start to keep a closer eye on a fund that is no longer as lustrous as it was when you were originally attracted to it. If your fund changes investing styles, and this doesn't suit your temperament, your risk tolerance, or your investing style, sell.

Recently, the mutual fund industry has had some difficulty retaining good managers. These hotshot managers like the free-style, less restricted world of hedge fund investing much better than the regulated, somewhat restricted mutual fund. The last thing you need to watch for is a change at the top. New managers, when they arrive on board, tend to revamp the old managers' holdings, which can cause a fund to lose some ground. Sometimes a little patience is worthwhile.

Just a side note about Jacob: His portfolio, after years of buying what's hot, is now littered with funds that essentially do the same thing. He is a collector of bright shiny things. Always trying to pluck the number one performer from the previous quarter, he has created a portfolio of funds that contains many of the same stocks, increasing his exposure and at the same time his risk.

Keeping your portfolio lean is incredibly important. A large number of funds do not create diversity. Too few funds in a portfolio present the opposite problem, not enough diversity. The magic number of funds for the average investor is usually six—one indexing the bond market, one indexing REITs, and four spread among equity indexes and actively managed funds.

Selling shares of a mutual fund is not as difficult as you might imagine. Often, if you want to keep the money in the same fund family, a telephone transfer from one fund to another is all it takes. If you decide that you would like to move your investments to another fund family, the new fund will provide you with the paperwork. Mutual funds inside a retirement account can't be sold without penalties. Don't be tempted in the changeover process to take some of the money out of your account.

Once the decision has been made, be comfortable with it. Selling your shares in a mutual fund is one way of voicing your dissatisfaction with the fund manager and his abilities.

Jacob, MaeLyn, and Talia need only keep a few things in mind when they invest in mutual funds. *Inflation matters.* In order for your dollar to be worth at least what it was when you invested it, it needs to return at least what inflation is. That is currently 2.5 percent.

No-load is always better than a load fund. Mark Carhart, who is currently doing quantitative research at Goldman Sachs, has found that the majority of funds that charge loads lag behind those that don't charge anything. And this, I understand, is before he calculated in the load fees those funds charge, sometimes in excess of 6 percent over the course of a decade.

Why do folks buy load funds in the first place? They believe in the sales pitch, the sales rep, and the hand holding, and once invested, they are unwilling to admit they made a mistake. On the surface, a load fund seems to perform better. It might be due to the lack of redemptions.

And then there's the holy trinity of successful investing—*exposure, risk,* and *diversity.* By holding a small number of funds spread out over various styles, you lessen your exposure to owning too much of the same thing, you spread the risk that all your investments will falter at the same time, and you attain diversity by participating in a number of different areas, increasing your chances for financial success.

DRAWING CONCLUSIONS

Jacob, our mutual fund collector, owned funds in three of the mutual fund families that came under investigation recently. This completely rattled him and caused some immediate paring of his holdings.

In case you weren't aware, New York Attorney General Eliot Spitzer found several high-profile mutual fund families involved in wrongdoing that literally involved stealing money from their own shareholders. As the tale unfolded, it became apparent that this problem was more widespread than originally anticipated.

The mutual fund industry had never experienced anything like this in its 80 years of servicing investors. While it was only pennies, when you consider the number of investors involved, those pennies added up to some significant dollars.

Investors like Jacob scurried for the door, even though restitution was made to the wronged investors.

- A popular investment seeking to steal some of the trillions of dollars invested in mutual funds are *exchange-traded funds*. These are index funds that trade throughout the day like stocks and can be bought or sold the same way. While they are gaining in popularity, these funds have some significant disadvantages.
- While they look like an index fund and charge similar low fees, profits from share increases are taxed as capital gains just like stocks. Brokers' fees and commissions will be charged at the purchase and again at the sale and should be calculated into your return.
- If you are investing in a 401(k) or 403(b) and your employer matches your contribution, do everything you can to make the minimum. This is free money that should be taken advantage of when offered.

10

Step 10: Now That You've Found Your Road, Stick to It

You should keep three words in mind as you approach your investments: *risk, reward,* and *reality.* Too much of one can cause your plan and your portfolio serious harm. To little of any one can find you just short of where you would like to be. In other words, the dose makes the poison. Before we get to the "where," let's look at some of the recommended daily dosages for the three R's of investing.

THE RIGHT BALANCE

Risk, as I have mentioned throughout the book, is and always will be one of the most difficult of the three to understand. We should all have a good idea of how risk works by this time. We tend to measure risk with a yardstick of balance. "Is it good for me?" we ask as we select the food we eat. "Is it safe?" we ask as we choose to drive instead of fly. "Is it pleasurable?" "Is it convenient?" "Is it hazardous?" we ask as we assess the worthiness of the effort. In investing, risk boils down to your ability to worry a little or worry a lot. The right balance of risks can mean that we might never need to worry at all.

The sad part is that we need to take on some risk just to stay even. That money in the cookie jar or under the mattress is still the same money in appearance, but inflation has taken its toll. That dollar stashed away losses value every day. Over the course of 10 or 20 years, that dollar, as we have found, can be worth considerably less because of inflation.

Squirreling away that money in a bank account, while safer, may not keep pace with inflation. If the return is less than the inflation rate, which at this writing is around the 2.5 percent range, you are not keeping pace—even without factoring in taxes. Thus it becomes a breakeven proposition. You need to be invested enough to beat inflation *and* taxes.

Faced with the question of "how much" risk you should take with your nest egg, we begin our search for the right balance between growing our money and sleeping comfortably. Too little risk will leave you with too small of a reward. Too much risk, and you might find yourself on the upside of increased wealth or, worse, the downside of a lost investment. This is when we realize that risk is forever intertwined with reward.

The cookie jar is a no-risk situation. It is also a no-reward choice. Small risk, small reward; the greater risk, the greater is the risk of reality. Why not the greater reward, you might ask.

Risk is always there. It is an ever-present reality of our lives from the minute we wake up until the time we go to bed at night. Too often, however, what we tend to ignore is the reality. When we decide to put our money to work, we need to understand that what we are doing is taking a chance.

Many of us know someone like my good friend Jeff. He eats and drinks organically, taking the best care of his body possible. He has, in his mind, eliminated much of the risk to a shorter life by taking care of himself. This does little to explain why Jeff jumps out of planes.

There is little real and tangible reward for this kind of risk. He would explain the thrill of the jump, the exhilaration of the free fall through space, or any number of superlatives that basically describe his risk as worth the effort to someone like me, a ground dweller. The only reward for those who are earth-bound is the safe landing. Relying on his parachute to open, doesn't he take risks far greater than the man who sits down to a 20-ounce T-bone steak night after night?

Investing is not that far removed from what Jeff does, at least on the surface. We should, as good investors, start with research. We should understand what we are trying to achieve. We are creatures that really need to understand the dangers we face on the ground and, more so, when we decide to "jump in" or, in Jeff's case, "jump out."

We can cull information from any number of resources, some paid for and some not. We weigh the pros and the cons, all the while asking ourselves if this is the right thing to do. As long as we question our motives, we will stick to the road we are on when it comes to investing. With our parachutes strapped to our backs, we take the plunge. As we free fall, we do either one or two things. We become exhilarated, the wind in our faces, the earth racing to meet us, pulling us with its gravity into its grasp. Or we worry.

We challenge this reality by understanding the risk and the reward. The real question lies in how we balance the three R's with certain times in our lives.

If you are a careful person, no amount of information will change what you are. To suggest that you should be, at an early age, taking great risks because of your far-reaching time horizon will fall on deaf ears. You are cautious, and you can hardly be expected to approach investing any differently.

A person who is willing to stare life squarely in the face each morning will pay little heed to someone like me when I suggest that you employ some conservatism when you invest. Therein lies the difficulty in reaching a balance. There are, however, some things that you should consider no matter what kind of person you are.

The one obstacle faced by blue-class investors is life. It tends to interrupt the best-laid plans and intentions. You get a job, and it seems that once that happens, the rest of your life should unfold in a somewhat predictable pattern. You might find yourself getting married, raising a family, and in the process, buying a house with all the trimmings. If you make an attempt to jump-start your savings for retirement before this all begins, you will be handsomely rewarded later.

But life will take it's own shape, almost treating us as passive participants. That's okay. If your savings and retirement plans are derailed while you are building a life for you and your loved ones, don't worry. That interruption is a worthwhile and rewarding experience in itself. You can restart your savings later in life, when things have calmed down a bit. That jump-start right from the beginning can give you an incredible advantage over those who wait though.

Even if you start out conservatively when you are young, you will win. Because of your age and that long investment road ahead of you, I wouldn't suggest that you do it that way, but the reward, while smaller, will still be there. Compounding will still work to your advantage.

No matter what your age, some portion of your portfolio should have exposure to both bonds and real estate investment trusts (REITs). I suggest that you keep 40 percent of your investable money in such places.

Indexing these two investments is the easiest way to allow you exposure while protecting the balance in your portfolio.

A beginning investor younger than age 40 should be thinking aggressively for the remaining 60 percent. How aggressive? I suggest *very* aggressive. This 60 percent of your portfolio will see the best return over those next 40 or 50 years when you begin early and aggressively. The buzzword here is *aggressive growth*.

So time rolls on. You either have continued investing, saving for your future by putting some money away in a retirement account (not enough to make you cash poor), or you have turned 40 without saving a dime. If you haven't taken advantage of your company's pension plan, if it even has a 401(k) or 403(b) plan, or if you haven't invested it in an IRA, now is the time to begin.

With the possibility that your work career can still span another 30 years, you technically still have a lot of time ahead of you. No need to panic. You probably have a house and have mostly raised your family, and even better, you have a much clearer understanding of who you are. Your financial partner and you can sit down and imagine how the plan should unfold. You can see the future a little more clearly.

This ability to imagine what might happen is something lost on youth. Those 20 years of maturity have given you foresight. The question is: What are you going to do with it?

If you are just getting into the game, the same 40 percent exposure to bonds and REITs in an indexed mutual fund is still wise. The need for some more conservative balance is still present. The remaining 60 percent, although still invested in growth, might find a little less aggressiveness in its content. Good, solid long-term performers in the growth area will do just the trick for your plan.

If you have a retirement plan at work, begin to invest as much as you can afford without making yourself cash poor. By hitting that adjustment just right, you avoid saving yourself right into debt. If you save too much, you won't have the cash necessary to get through life's little obstacles. If you don't save enough, you will be tempted to spend the excess cash. This is when paying yourself first becomes incredibly important.

If your investment plan provides a match, take advantage of it. This is free money. Many companies are rethinking a good many pension plans across the country, and this idea of a company match has come under scrutiny as a way to cut costs. Some companies have eliminated it or greatly reduced the options under which they provide those matching funds. This doesn't make a pension plan less important to your future, just a little less lucrative.

If you do not have a retirement account at work that deducts pretax income from your pay, you need to seek out your own account. Traditional IRAs, a plan that allows you to deduct any contribution made to it during a calendar year from your income taxes, is an excellent beginning. In many cases, mutual fund families will offer IRA investors a break on getting started. Sometimes it is a low initial deposit to open the account and sometimes lower minimum contributions afterward. At the end of this chapter, I will list a few funds that offer such breaks for retirement investors.

While a traditional IRA allows you to deduct contributions from your taxes, a Roth IRA allows you to save for retirement in the same way with one difference: The money you have contributed has already been taxed. When you retire or begin withdrawing this money, all the contributions you made throughout the years are tax-free. You only pay taxes on the interest accrued. Roth IRAs are excellent sources of retirement savings for folks who have defined benefit pension plans where they work.

By the time you have reached 50 years of age, and with any luck you have been investing diligently throughout your career, those growth funds should be moved gradually into more conservative index funds. With more than half your working career over, you should be entering into a more pro-tection-oriented mind-set. At least half of your 60 percent portfolio in equity funds should reflect this more conservative approach. Leave one or two funds invested in growth while moving the other half of your invest-ments into something more balanced. Be careful, though. You want to be careful that this conservatism doesn't change your 60/40 split. Some bal-anced funds use bonds as their method for achieving that evenness. Look for funds that are still in equities (stocks) but invest in more solid compa-nies perhaps paying dividends.

At age 60, your fund allocation should be split in the other direction. Instead of 60 percent in equities and 40 percent in bond and REIT indexes, the balance should reverse itself. You should be 60 percent in bond and REIT indexes and 40 percent involved in conservative equities. While some people disagree with those percentages at that age, I believe that the majority of Americans, those who are the blue class, will still be gainfully employed. They may have found little need to slow down and stop working or have switched to part time. This assumption should be taken one step further.

By age 60, it might be safe to assume that your house is paid for, and you have a clear vision of how your retirement will unfold and what you will want (or be capable of) doing. That dream of traveling the world you entertained at age 25 may have mellowed into something less dramatic. Your dream may be lakeside fishing or chasing a golf ball around your favorite public course.

A MORE RELAXED INVESTOR

If you pay too close attention to what the markets are doing on a daily basis, you will cause yourself more anxiety than it is worth. Folks, who pay close attention to what is happening on a day-to-day basis begin to believe that they can time the markets. Few folks are able to do this without the assistance of vast research teams, singular analytical skills, and a fully functioning crystal ball. The ability to put your money in during a down market so as to take advantage of depressed prices is an incredibly difficult skill to have. Investing regularly and steadily (dollar-cost averaging) will reap the most rewards. You will be able to take advantage of those lower prices when they are available without the added stress.

This is not to say that you shouldn't open those statements when they arrive. In times of market turmoil, the temptation simply to drop those quarterly envelopes in a drawer unopened is often overwhelming. Open them, examine them, and try to understand why your fund manager has failed to succeed to your expectations. Compare your fund's returns with those of its peer group, not some popular index. If you are indexed, you should have returns that mimic the index. If not, ask why.

Life is meant to be enjoyed. Far too much pressure is put on making you believe that retirement is the time of your life. *Now* is the time of your life. If you make an attempt to save money for your retirement, you will be that much farther ahead. In the mean time, enjoy your family, have a barbecue, go fishing, coach a kid's sports team, read, explore volunteerism, learn a craft, or take a class. Just save something. For most of America, life will intrude, and while it may be a welcome intrusion in most cases, it will still be a distraction. If you begin a plan, stay with it in principle. By being flexible, you can tailor the plan to your current needs. If the kids need braces, that contribution to your IRA may be less this year. Just be sure that you make some sort of payment to yourself.

For many blue-class investors—and I am one myself—savings will not make you rich, but it will enrich you.

DRAWING CONCLUSIONS

Here are some final thoughts to keep in mind. Social Security, unless revamped by a committed White House and Congress, will face difficulties in the years ahead. Keep this in mind when electing officials to represent you.

The average working man will receive a little over $1000 in benefits when he retires; a woman will receive just shy of $800.

- Pensions can be broken down into two distinct categories. Defined benefit plans are sponsored by your employer, who selects an administrator to invest those funds for you. When you retire, you receive a fixed monthly benefit.

- In defined contribution plans—401(k) plans for private-sector workers and 403(b) plans for public employees—you provide the investment funds for your retirement. These contributions are taken from your paycheck before taxes. Unlike defined benefit plans, these pensions are not insured, but the choice of investments is usually yours to make. These plans are also portable, allowing you to take them with you should you change jobs. These types of pensions can be rolled over into IRAs should you decide to retire or are employed by a company that has no plan available. I can't stress the importance of using these plans to fund your retirement. A defined contribution pension plan's success rests squarely on your shoulders.

- A traditional IRA is a tax-deferred retirement account that is used by individuals where no other pension plan is offered. You can con-

tribute up to $3000 a year into this account and $3500 a year if
you are age 50 or older.

- A Roth IRA can be used by anyone, even if they have a pension
  at work. The contribution you make to this plan has already been
  taxed. The same contribution limits for the traditional IRA apply
  here also.

GLOSSARY

MORTGAGE TERMS

Adjustable-rate mortgage (ARM) A mortgage loan subject to changes in interest rates usually based on prime rates, and when those rate indexes change, your ARM monthly payments increase or decrease at preset intervals determined by the lender. The change in monthly payment amount, however, is usually subject to a cap, and the whole loan itself is usually convertible to a fixed rate.

Amortization The actual repayment of a mortgage loan through monthly installments of principal and interest. Your monthly payment amount is based on a schedule that will allow you to own your home at the end of a specific time period (often 15 or 30 years).

Annual percentage rate (APR) The APR shows the cost of a loan. This is calculated using a standard formula. This number is often expressed as a yearly interest rate, including the interest, points, mortgage insurance, etc. that may be associated with the loan.

Assumable mortgage A mortgage that can be transferred from a seller to a buyer, freeing the seller from any obligation on the home when it passes the loan onto the buyer.

Cap A limit, such as that placed on an ARM, on how much a monthly payment or interest rate can increase or decrease.

Cash reserves Sometimes this is called a down payment that the lender may require that also can be used for closing costs.

Closing costs This little bill is above and beyond the sale price of a property and must be paid to cover the transfer of ownership at closing. These costs can vary widely from place to place.

Conventional loan This is often considered a private-sector loan, which is not guaranteed or insured by the U.S. government.

Credit history A history of your debt payments. It is used by lenders to gauge your ability to repay a loan and to determine the best rate of interest.

Credit report Your credit "report card," which is a black and white, and sometimes red, accounting that lists all past and present debts and the timeliness of their repayment. It is your credit history laid bare.

Credit bureau score Used to determine your ability to qualify for a mortgage loan and, of course, if the loan is approved, whether you might, somewhere in the future, default.

Debt-to-income ratio Determines how much of a direct burden your debts are to your income. It is a comparison of gross income to housing and nonhousing expenses. If you are using the Federal Housing Administration (FHA) to purchase your home, the monthly mortgage payment should be no more than 29 percent of your monthly gross income (before taxes), and the mortgage payment combined with nonhousing debts should not exceed 41 percent of your income. This is standard throughout the industry.

Deed A document that signifies the final transfer of ownership of a property from the lender or seller to you.

Delinquency The failure of a borrower to make timely mortgage payments under a loan agreement.

Discount point *Points,* as these are sometimes called, can be used to purchase a loan at a lower interest rate.

Down payment A payment, usually cash, to bring down the cost of a loan itself.

Earnest money Cash that tells the seller that you are indeed serious about purchasing a home. If the offer is accepted, it becomes part of the down payment. If the seller doesn't like the deal and rejects your offer, the money is returned. If you back out of the deal once the offer has been made, however, you lose any money in the account.

Energy Efficient Mortgage (EEM) An FHA program that helps home buyers save money on utility bills by enabling them to finance the cost of adding energy-efficiency features to a new or existing home as part of the home purchase.

Equity The difference between what you owe on your mortgage and what your property is worth.

Escrow account A separate account into which the lender puts a portion of each monthly mortgage payment that has been calculated to cover expenses such as property taxes, homeowners' insurance, mortgage insurance, etc.

Fair Housing Act A law that prohibits discrimination in the home-buying process on the basis of race, color, national origin, religion, sex, familial status, or disability.

Fair market value The agreed-on price of a property.

Fannie Mae The Federal National Mortgage Association (FNMA) is not a government agency but is a federally chartered enterprise owned by private stockholders. The purpose of this company is to purchase residential mortgages and convert them into securities for sale to investors.

FHA The Federal Housing Administration was established in 1934 to advance homeownership opportunities for all Americans. It still assists in this process by providing home buyers' mortgage insurance to lenders to cover most losses that may occur when a borrower defaults. This helps to encourage lenders to make loans to borrowers who might not otherwise qualify for conventional mortgages. To learn more about the FHA, visit its Web site (*http://www.hud.gov/*) or write the FHA at the U.S. Department of Housing and Urban Development, 451 7th Street, S.W., Washington, DC 20410. Telephone: (202) 708-1112; TTY: (202)708-1455.

Fixed-rate mortgage Mortgages with payments that remain the same throughout the life of the loan because the interest rate and other terms are fixed and do not change.

Foreclosure The legal process in which a mortgaged property is sold to pay the loan of a defaulting borrower. According to Housing and Urban Development (HUD), there are three things you should do to avoid this happening: (1) *Do not ignore the letters from your lender.* (If you are having problems making your payments, call or write to your lender's loss mitigation department without delay.) (2) *Stay in your home.* (You may not qualify for assistance if you leave the residence.) (3) Contact a HUD-approved housing counseling agency or call (800) 569-4287 or TDD (800) 877-8339 for the housing counseling agency nearest you.

Freddie Mac The Federal Home Loan Mortgage Corporation (FHLM) is another federally chartered corporation and publicly held company that purchases residential mortgages.

Ginny Mae The Government National Mortgage Association (GNMA) provides a link between capital markets (the lenders) and the federal housing markets. Ninety-five percent of all home loans through the Federal Housing Authority (FHA) and the Veterans Administration (VA) are backed by GNMA.

Good-faith estimate An estimate of all closing fees, including prepaid and escrow items and lender charges. This must be given to a borrower within 3 days of submission of a loan application.

HUD The U.S. Department of Housing and Urban Development was established in 1965 and works to create a decent home and suitable living environment for all Americans. It accomplishes this by addressing housing needs, improving and developing American communities, and enforcing fair housing laws.

HUD1 statement Also known as the *settlement sheet,* largely because it itemizes all the closing costs in a real estate sale. Rules say that this sheet must be given to the borrower at or before the closing.

Interest rate Literally the cost of the money you are about to borrow. This is the tax-deductible attraction to homeownership.

Lease purchase Creates an opportunity for low- to moderate-income renters to become low- to moderate-income home buyers by allowing these tenants to become owners if they so desire. The rent payment is made up of the monthly rental payment plus an additional amount that is credited to an account for use as a down payment.

Lien A legal claim against a property that must be satisfied before the property can be sold so that the deed comes to the closing "clean."

Loan-to-value (LTV) ratio Establishes the amount of a down payment needed. Expressed as a percentage, it is calculated by dividing the amount borrowed by the price or appraised value of the home to be purchased.

Mortgage In it's basic form, a mortgage is a lien on a property that secures the promise that you will fulfill your end of the deal and repay a loan.

Principal The actual loan amount excluding interest.

Title insurance Used by a lender to protect against any claims that arise from arguments about ownership of a property.

Truth in Lending Act A federal law for your protection obligating a lender to give a full written disclosure of all fees, terms, and conditions associated with a loan's initial period.

VA Department of Veterans Affairs guarantees loans made to veterans, usually at favorable rates and terms.

INSURANCE TERMS

Accelerated-benefits rider Allows an insured to receive early payment of some portion of a policy's face amount should the insured suffer from a terminal illness or injury.

Accidental death benefit rider A rider that covers accidental death, providing additional cash based on your untimely demise.

Annual beneficiary The person(s) who receives the payment for your life insurance policy. If you have a will, it should be listed "as per will."

Cap Your total out-of-pocket expense for your policy during the course of a year, usually in reference to health insurance.

Cash value In a whole-life insurance policy, this accumulation can be used to pay premiums long after many policies have lapsed.

Collision coverage Collision coverage helps to pay auto repair or replacement costs if your car hits another vehicle or an object.

Comprehensive coverage Covers damage to your car resulting from fire, some natural disasters, falling objects, vandalism, and theft.

Convertible term insurance Term insurance that can be exchanged (converted) at the option of the policy owner and without evidence of insurability for a permanent insurance policy.

Copayment A flat fee paid when medical service is received.

COBRA Stands for Consolidated Omnibus Budget Reconciliation Act. This federal law, passed in 1985, made it possible for workers and their covered spouses and children to remain on a former employer's health care plan for a set period of time.

Death benefit The amount of money paid to a beneficiary when the insured person dies. See *Beneficiary*.

Decreasing-term insurance Term life insurance on which the face value slowly decreases in scheduled steps from the date the policy comes into force to the date the policy expires, while the premium remains level.

Deductible Simply, the higher the deductible, the lower is the premium on an insurance policy.

Depreciation The decline in an object's value due to age, wear and tear, or obsolescence.

Dividend A return of part of the premium on participating insurance that is based on the insurer's investment, mortality, and expense experience. Dividends are not guaranteed and should be reinvested.

Evidence of insurability Any statement or proof of a person's physical condition, occupation, etc. that affects the acceptance of the applicant for insurance.

Exclusions What the insurance company won't pay. Of course, for a price, it can cover these specified hazards that are otherwise listed in a policy as benefits that will not be paid.

Face amount or value The amount stated on the face of an insurance policy that will be paid in case of death.

Fixed benefit A death benefit, the dollar amount of which does not vary.

Grace period The period after the due date of a premium during which the policy remains in force without penalty.

Guaranteed term A form of renewable term insurance that remains in force as long as the premiums are paid on time.

Health maintenance organization (HMO) Paid by monthly premium, an HMO covers services such as doctors' visits, hospital stays, etc. The HMO designates doctors and hospitals.

Indemnity A predetermined sum paid for a covered loss.

Liability A term that broadly means legal responsibility.

Occupational hazard Whether it is a type of job or a workplace problem, it is a condition in an occupation that increases the chance of accident, sickness, or death.

Permanent (life insurance) Any form of life insurance except term that builds up a cash value, such as whole life.

Preexisting condition A health problem that existed or for which the insured received treatment before the date health care insurance became effective.

Premiums Payments to an insurance company to buy a policy and to keep it in force.

Rider An attachment to a policy that modifies or changes the policy's conditions by expanding.

Risk The chance of injury, damage, or loss.

Term insurance Life insurance that does not build up cash value and where the premium remains the same for the life of the policy.

Third-party owner A policy owner who is not the insured.

Underwriter A company receiving premiums and accepting responsibility for fulfilling a policy contract.

Universal life insurance A flexible premium life insurance policy under which the policy owner may change the death benefit based on the amount of premium they pay. The death benefit can change if the premium increases or decreases.

Whole-life insurance A basic type of permanent life insurance that can provide lifetime protection at a level premium. Premiums generally must be paid for as long as the policy is in force.

Index

About the Author

Paul Petillo was raised in the Philadelphia area. He moved to the west coast after extensive travel across the United States and Europe, started a family in Portland, Oregon in the early eighties, and is now blessed with three sons and a daughter, two "favorite" daughters-in-law, and two grand-sons.

He is currently employed as a meat manager for Fred Meyer, a large northwest grocery chain owned by Kroger. He has been with the company for 27 years, twenty of those in management and has worked in the meat industry for 36 years. He is also a union member with UFCW Local 555 in Portland.

Paul began writing at an early age, but with the creation of the BlueCollarDollar in 1998 he found his niche. He created a financial education site devoted to a common sense approach to money, investing and retirement. It was designed to be a personal exploration of the world of money and how it affects our wallets. In 2002, he created the BlueMoney Report, a widely syndicated online commentary on money, Wall Street, and Washington.